The Bridge That Carries You Over

MIKE LUNSFORD

Best wishes,

Shade Tree Press

8945 South Coxville Rd.

Rosedale, Indiana 47874

www.mikelunsford.com

Printed in the United States of America

The author and publisher gratefully acknowledges the *Terre Haute Tribune-Star* in which the contents of this book appeared in column form.

Library of Congress Control Number: 2015908959

Front and back cover art by Mike Lunsford. Inside cover art, *Spring in Parke County* by D. Omer Seamon, is courtesy of Rose-Hulman Institute of Technology. Back cover author's photo by Joan Lunsford.

Lunsford, Michael J. (Mike), 1956-
The Bridge That Carries You Over/Mike Lunsford
ISBN 978-0-692-46301-7 (pbk.)

To my friends, who have been my bridges. And to my grandson, Daniel Gilbert Lunsford, who was born on nearly the same day as this book: May you be as fortunate in life as your grandparents have been...

-Preface-

I am writing this on an extraordinarily cool late spring day, the kind that I lean toward most of all since there is a breeze straining itself through my open windows, the birds are at my feeders, and a half-dozen or so dragonflies are playing tag near my doorstep. It is a quiet day, just right for writing and thinking, and napping, the latter at which I uncharacteristically failed to accomplish about an hour ago.

This is my fifth collection of stories, one which I said I wouldn't put together until I had written a childhood memoir of sorts that has been living in my head for years now. But here the collection comes anyway, being shoved out the door not unlike what poet Anne Bradstreet once called her work: "a poorly-dressed child." As usual, it is up to you to tell me whether you like it or not.

The title of this book comes from the story I have placed at its very beginning. I have not given the title to you in its entirety, not only because of limited space on the cover and the inside title page, but because by shortening it I have neutralized its early command to "Thank the bridge." Now, I am simply asking you to recall those people and events that have been the bridges that have carried you across and through tough times. We've all had them.

Bridges are an absolute necessity where I live. In my very rural, very green Indiana county, we have so many creeks and runs and branches that years and years ago we began to build bridges out of necessity, for we are notoriously known for our floods, and the fording of most streams here became quite impractical, no matter how stout your horses or Model T's were. Many of those bridges crossed rather wide and brown and muddy creeks like the Big Raccoon and Sugar Creek and Leatherwood Creek, and even the great Wabash River near places like Montezuma and Clinton. Many of our bridges, however, also cross "runs," like the one no more than a mile or so from where I sit right now. Originally called Iron Run for its reddish, rust-tinted water, it eventually became Rock Run. I can nearly spit across that creek in August, but get enough rain and a bit of winter snow melt, and Rock Run fills itself from bank to bank. One of my favorite bridges, the Harry Evans Bridge, takes visitors from one patch of gravel there to the other.

A great number of our bridges are covered bridges, most often seen in picturesque New England landscapes, but built here in even greater numbers because of the distances between our small towns and a proclivity, I am told, for our rich soils to produce yellow poplar, the wood of choice when it comes to bridges and barns and fences, even outhouses.

The Harry Evans Bridge is one of those tin-roofed masterpieces, and I live less than two miles from several longer bridges, both double-Burr Arched. I swam under and near them when I was a boy, fished around them with my grandfather, who is the subject of a favored but unpublished story that will serve as a final bookend to this collection.

There is a natural link between these real bridges of the present and the people who have been important parts of my life. Many of the great adventures of my childhood came by riding in the bed of a pick-up truck for a Sunday afternoon near or under a bridge, and it was in those places that I got to know more about the land I lived on, nearly as much as the people I lived with.

There is much to be said about spending time alone with a creek, or a sandbar and its cottonwood trees and mussels, the smell of green in your nostrils and the feel of mud under your feet. I certainly wish more parents encouraged it with their children. It is a treat that I wanted my children to experience, and they did, and I truly believe their time, often alone in the woods and near streams taught them more than any classroom or teacher ever could. They have come to care for the land and for the creatures that inhabit it; they too have felt and seen the simple beauty that a handful of wet gravel possesses, know the awesome construction of leaves and seeds, appreciate the architecture of anthills and bird nests and hornets' paper. I have every intention of making that sort of education happen for my grandchildren too, that is when they themselves happen…

So, for the most part, the stories you are about to read are about my bridges—the people and places that have helped me through troubled times, for sure, but also stood by as I celebrated and enjoyed the best of times too. Good friends, quiet places, a mate for life, loving children and grandchildren, these are the bridges worth building and appreciating.

As you will soon discover in my first story, "Thank the bridge that carries you over," is an old Scottish adage, one I often used to mutter just after passing across an ancient concrete bridge that spanned the Big Raccoon near a little stop-in-the-road called Armiesburg, a few miles from my place. I said it because the bridge, which has now been replaced with much fanfare and considerable inconvenience and money, appeared as though it had stood on its last arthritic legs for the past 20 years or so. I was just thankful that each time I, or my wife, or a school bus load of my students made it from one side of that often-flooded ravine to the other, that the bridge had done its job. Hopefully, like that old bridge, we are allowed to stick around long enough to serve a lot of people, a helpful hand as others work their way through life.

I have a few bridges to thank just in getting this book out, and I don't mean those made of concrete or poplar. The good people at the *Terre Haute Tribune-Star* continue to let me use front page space for my writing, and for that, I continue to thank them. And, of course, there is my wife, Joanie; she's been the best bridge I could ever have.

-Table of Contents-

We shall not cease from exploration
And the end of all our exploring
Will be to arrive where we started
And know the place for the first time.

T.S. Eliot

I still find each day too short for all the thoughts I want to think, all the walks I want to take, all the books I want to read, and all the friends I want to see.

John Burroughs

I suppose that a writer, almost by definition, is a person incapable of satisfaction—which is what keeps him at his post.

E.B. White

The Bridge That Carries You Over

Shade Tree Press

The Bridge That Carries You Over

Despite a surprising and peaceful November snow that fell on the other side of my window last Sunday, I struggled mightily to think of a story to write for this day, one of the few that is yet to be played out before Thanksgiving comes.

Although it appeared to be an easy chore, I had written so often in the past about the holiday that it seemed my trouble was a simple lack of creative spark, not one of a loss of gratitude, that bothered me most.

That morning, my minister announced to our congregation that he looked forward to reading my annual Thanksgiving offering. Little did he know that I was at that very moment completely preoccupied in the doodling and scratching of notes on our church bulletin, glassy-eyed as I meandered through ideas for that very piece.

He met me at the door as we filed out to tell me that he lives a little "vicariously" through my words. Well, the time has come for him to read them, and I hope he is not to be disappointed.

By midday, despite a desire to just forget about writing altogether and wait for a "Eureka Moment" to strike, perhaps by halftime of the Green Bay-Philadelphia game, I sat in the dark warmth of our family room, the competing purrs of forced heated air and our black house cat pushing me toward stupor. And then it came to me.

There is an old Scottish saying that goes something

3

like this: "Thank the bridge that carries you over." The adage just popped into my head, apparently on the loose from some cobwebbed and dusty cerebral storage room, and it was soon apparent that it would remain foremost in my mind until I wrote it down or wrote about it.

Although I have been on my share of decrepit county bridges — those that looked as if they stood on their last legs, ones that surely the next high water or too-heavy load would bring down — they have delivered me to the other side of the creek, and for that I have been thankful.

But to me, that old saying carries more weight than any real bridge: We must be thankful for the people who have helped us get across the creek, too.

It would be an arrogant and errant message to suggest that I can name everyone who has given me a hand, believed in me, helped me in some way in the half-century or so that I have been breathing. I imagine that no matter how long you search the recesses of your own memories, the same is true for you, as well.

Of course, I can thank the usual suspects, such as my parents, who between them had only a single high school diploma and the calloused hands and bent backs of labor and wait. My grandparents, on both sides of the family lived similarly.

My maternal grandfather died at 38, still working in the coal mines that ruined his health; my step-grandfather, a hard-working meat cutter, lived only a year after finally attaining what he wanted to do more than anything else in his life: own a country grocery store.

My grandmothers, both scrimpers and savers, also lived too-short lives, and my Grandfather Roy, that feisty and stubborn hero of many of my tales, seems to still whisper in my ear, particularly if I am up against a thing I don't believe I can budge, no matter how hard I push.

We all have had them: sisters and brothers, stepmothers and foster parents, grandparents and crazy uncles, and if we're lucky, as I have been, a wife or husband who has always been there for us.

Of course, there have been teachers, including those rare ones who believed in me more than I did in myself, those who, on occasion, had the fortitude to spank my bottom, and a few more who offered a ride home, an encouraging word, a listening ear.

There have been friends, the best who bothered to call or stop by the house when they thought I'd needed it, those who knew me best, but liked me anyway. Some who sat with me in the watch cares of hospital waiting rooms, others who danced at our family weddings, celebrated with us at the birth of our babies, sent in food in times of illness, offered a hug or bothered to mail a card when we grieved or ailed. There have been co-workers, too, people who have listened when I complained, given advice, shared experience, showed me a way.

And then there are the countless and nameless souls

who lent their backs to help push a ditched car, gave a dime when I didn't have it, cared when they didn't have to, complimented when it wasn't required, proved thoughtful when others walked by. They've pointed the way in strange places, given me the time, opened a door, offered help, given a break... And for them, I am thankful, too.

On my worst days, I halfway come to the conclusion that squander has replaced mercy in this hypercritical and more mean-spirited world we have made, that common sense is dying, that the only thing we can do is fight in the hardscrabble to make a way for ourselves and our families. Yet I am a firm believer in what the historian David McCullough has said: "There is no such thing as a self-made man."

Whatever I am — whatever we all are — is perhaps less about what we have inside us, but rather about what the people around us had and have in them.

And for that, I am thankful.

On the Good of Being Outdoors

I went to the window first thing last Sunday morning, wild-haired and sleepy-eyed, my unshaven face pressed near the glass to see if it had frosted.

It had, and I could tell by the cold white comforter that lay on the grass that the first hard freeze of the year had arrived like Carl Sandburg's fog, "on little cat feet," quietly and stealthily.

I had gone to bed feeling good about the yard work I had accomplished the afternoon before. Although I know much more labor is yet to be invested, I had raked and mowed and tarped and trimmed myself silly, just to see for a little while that my grass was still green underneath the newly-laid carpet of maple and poplar leaves.

A fresh kind of neatness had transformed my place just a few hours after I had begun the work, but I suspected that it would take no more than a night of breeze to bring chaos to my newly wrought order.

The whole scene was so pretty that I walked down my drive to watch the sun drop toward the horizon; it cast my efforts in a nearly horizontal and pleasing light.

It was eye-wateringly clear and windy all day that day, but since the squirrels and a bit of windy Halloween-night snow had wreaked havoc on our jack-o'-lanterns, and had strewn limbs about like gray-brown confetti, I decided to do a bit of cleaning up and throwing away.

After all, most of our flower pots held only the limp and hollow dregs of the dead and dying; our chrysanthemums drooped like bent old men, and my gutters were stuffed with leaves.

So I ventured outside, gloved and long-johned, to fight the fight, and was glad I did, for the work eventually warmed me in more than one way. My weekday job is one that often saddles me to a desk chair like a cowboy to his mount, and over the week I had grown achy and unmotivated, and I felt old.

The feel of sunshine and the earthy scent and color of the leaves gave me a sense of purpose. I actually resented having to come indoors by the time it was growing dark, despite the backache that always accompanies my use of hand rakes.

When my wife emerged from the cocoon of our bedroom, a bit disheveled and half-asleep herself, I made the announcement about the frost as if a major news story had broken. The night before, we had monitored the dipping numbers of our car thermometer as it had dropped a degree or two at a time on the drive home from town.

"You can hardly tell you cleaned up the yard," she said as she staggered on to a rendezvous with a bathroom mirror.

My yard is an expansive work-in-progress. At a time when I should be finding ways to make it smaller, it seems to grow a little each year as I clean a corner or fence row; my children have begun to question my sanity.

It has taken years, but I have cut down or trimmed many of our less desirable trees. As loath as I am to cutting a tree, I have replaced all those I have disposed of in spades.

Although I still have three big old silver maples running south to north across my yard, I have planted scarlet pin oaks and yellow poplars and orange maples and yellow magnolias here and there.

The magnolia was a brilliant ball of lemon-colored leaves when I took that last walk down my drive that day. But when I awoke, hardly a leaf remained in place; the frost, as Frost the poet once wrote, decapitated them in "accidental power."

I do a lot of thinking while I do yard work; it is the kind of mental exercise I need. It's more like stretching one's muscles than working them, to keep the metaphor going.

For instance, I have been contemplating getting rid of my old cell phone, so part of my raking time was spent in the consideration of trading it for a newer, slicker bit of technology that would leave email and web searches much closer to me than where I can find them now.

I don't need a new phone, don't even mind that those around me think I am some sort of technological Neanderthal, either. I don't even like to speak on the phone, and I never carry mine in a jeans pocket while I work. In fact, I was enjoying myself in the yard having no one to speak to, no phones, no texts, no news updates.

By lunchtime that day, Joanie had told me that she had all the costs of acquiring the new phone figured out. It took her, by the way, about 45 minutes on her phone to get an answer

But with all things considered, I think I'll keep my old piece of technology; I just can't justify my dalliance with more ease and convenience and social acceptance for the investment it requires.

Not long ago, I read a piece by *New York Times* columnist Nicholas Kristof, who like me, often writes about man's interaction — or rather the lack of it — with nature. Unlike me, however, he has won a Pulitzer Prize.

In "Blissfully Lost in the Woods," Kristof wrote of the 10 days he and his daughter spent hiking the Pacific Coast Trail in Oregon. Although never in any real danger, they were lost much of the time, and were so without cell phone reception.

"In our modern society," he wrote, "we have structured the world to obey us; we can often use a keyboard or remote to alter our surroundings. Yet all this gadgetry focused on our comfort doesn't always leave us more content or grounded." Later, he wrote: "Perhaps wilderness is an antidote to our postindustrial self-absorption... trudging uphill through mosquito swarms isn't for everyone. But unplugging long enough to encounter nature is less scary and more fortifying than people may expect."

A weekend in the yard — with an extra foray into the woods to admire the falling leaves — was hardly backpacking with the bears, but from the too-little time I have to walk my walk or sit in my woods, or to even spend with a rake in my hands, I have come to think the same thing. Don't bother calling to convince me otherwise.

The Things We'd Carry, Carry Memories

Although I have a "to read" stack in my old breezeway office that is taller than I am, I have been in the mood lately to re-read a few books that I haven't had my nose into for years.

I hate to admit, particularly since I just had another birthday, that several of those old favorites seem almost entirely new to me now. But I'm enjoying them all over again, and that's one of the reasons I have such a hard time getting rid of books.

Just a few days ago, I picked up Harper Lee's *To Kill a Mockingbird*, which I haven't read since high school. I want to teach it to two of my classes this year, and I can't say that I remember it well enough to try without re-reading it first. I am reliving that book — actually appreciating it much more this time around — and I hope my students come to love Lee's words and ideas as I do, especially if it means they'll read it again in a few decades. I experienced the same thing last spring as I read Willa Cather's *My Antonia*. What a wonderful book it is.

I keep favorite books on my cabin desktop, not only for their looks and feel and scent, but simply to keep them in mind. E.B. White's collected essays are there (essential reading, in my opinion, to anyone who ever dreamed of calling himself a writer).

Robert Louis Stevenson occupies two spots: Once with *Treasure Island*, and again with *Kidnapped*. Those books still appeal to the boyheart in me, and I'd say that sometime this winter I'll be reading them again, perhaps one night when a cold wind is driving snow against the side of the house, and I am appreciating both a blanket and a fire.

Before this reverie broke in, I'd wanted to say that I need to re-read Tim O'Brien's *The Things They Carried*, which has been on my mind since I spotted it hiding on a shelf a few weeks ago.

Written nearly 25 years ago, it is an anthology of sorts, a series of short stories about a platoon's experiences in Vietnam. It is not necessarily a fun book to read, for it puts pictures in my head that I'd rather not live with for long. The men in O'Brien's somewhat autobiographical novel carried all kinds of things into the jungles with them, from Bibles to love letters, but the things they took away from their time there are much less innocent.

A year and a half ago, Connie Schultz actually planted this story's idea in my head. She wrote a short piece for "Parade" magazine — which this newspaper includes in its Sunday editions — and in it she pondered five things she'd "carry" away from her house if she ever had to run from fire or flood. In other words, what five things would she do her best to hang onto forever? It is a much more difficult question to answer than I first thought. I went in search of folks who had that same question to answer, and I wasn't surprised to learn that many would grab their phones and laptops, their pets, even favorite shoes and family genealogy records.

Like Schultz, I have come to the conclusion that the things I'd "carry" from my home would be very personal, things that in most cases, I imagine, wouldn't be worth much to others at all. As I run through my short list, I hope you'll consider what you'd keep, for I hardly think I'm the only sentimental fool around.

Perhaps the first thing I'd carry is my dad's Case pocketknife; in fact, I carry it all the time. I never knew him not to have a knife in his pocket, and he always encouraged me to have one in mine, too.

Although he occasionally carried a Buck or Schrade, Dad was always partial to Cases, those made with amber bone and American steel. Since his passing, 18 years ago now, I have replaced the one he gave to me when I was hardly 10 or so with the last knife he owned.

I am lucky to still have it, considering I lost it once near New Salem, Ill., on a bus tour. It was found and miraculously made its way back into my pocket, where I hope it will stay for a long, long time yet.

My mom's Bible has to come along with me, too. Mom never carried a grand leather model that was rarely opened, but rather an inexpensive paper-bound student Bible, eventually held together by packing tape; it is filled with comments and observations she'd written in its margins.

I can still see my mother in its pages, her beautiful

handwriting penciled here and there and filling the blank pages near the back. In one spot, she had written, "No one is rich unless he has friends ..."

I dreamed of being an archaeologist when I was a boy, and for that reason, one of the arrowheads I found while scrabbling in the sandy soil of my childhood home place nearly a half-century ago has to be my third treasure.

I have kept the point on a shelf for years, and each time I see it there, I still see myself in short pants and white T-shirt, my knees skinned and arms scrawny.

My life as a kid was one of exploration and discovery, all in a few square acres of woods and dry creek beds; that arrowhead takes me back to all of it.

My grandmother's diary makes the list, too. It is a small brown dime store affair and includes the final words she ever wrote. Its entries are remarkably simple, mostly observations on the weather and a list of chores she'd tackled each day. To find my name tucked into her diaries brings back a floodtide of what Scott Sanders once called the "persistent presence of memory." I will read that diary again and again.

I have tried very hard for years now to scan and digitally store about every photograph that means much to us, but one frame of pictures we have hanging on our living room wall would have to come out with me, too, because, for some reason, I have not touched it since I first drove a nail into the wall.

One photo in particular is of my daughter, who at two or so had been playing in our back yard near our hydrant. I remember that I had been working on a fence that spring day more than 30 years ago, and Ellen, in bibbed overalls and striped shirt, is chubby and blonde and laughing. She is covered in mud from head to toe, loving the feel of water and grit between her fingers, and everything was new and possible to her.

How could I ever leave that behind?

It Isn't the End, but It Is the Beginning of the End...

I had every intention of writing about Labor Day today; it has become a tradition of sorts for me because it seems as though my column and the holiday have an annual convergence. But as I thumbed through a number of other stories I'd written on the subject, I felt I had nothing new to say. Ironically, it seemed just too much work to start on another.

But, one thing that I have considered lately is how Labor Day marks the end of the real summer, some three weeks or so ahead of whatever the calendar says. Years ago, of course, we never went back to school until after Labor Day, and so it seemed more like fall by then. I miss that. Now, August has barely begun, and so has school with its grading, lesson plans and assignments, and its early-morning face-shaving and tooth-brushing and alarm clock grumbling.

In just the past few days, despite this late-arriving heat wave we've all panted through, I have seen signs that the summer is nearly spent; autumn and its cooler breezes can't be far off. Already, I have watched leaves lazily drift out of my hackberry tree near the mouth of my drive, leaving a skimpy and noticeable smattering of crunchy yellow that is milled under the tires of our car. My wife and I have pinched our chrysanthemums' buds back all summer long to keep them from blooming early, but now we see flashes of orange and crimson out of them, and this time, we are letting them go.

I have also noticed that many of the tall grasses — those that I have growing about my yard, and those that stand along the roadsides that have managed to elude the mowers and sprayers — are seeding themselves with heavy heads.

Despite the recent dry weeks and our want for a soaking rain, those stands of grass just do what they are supposed to do, when they are supposed to do it.

Perhaps I am just anxious to drag out long-sleeved shirts and rakes and firewood, but it takes no special skill to find subtle signs of the inevitable. For instance, we've had a particularly vocal and abundant cricket population around our place all summer, but in recent weeks it has become an all-out assault on our home. Every night, we see them hopping from point to point in our garage, probing our defenses, attempting to send agents across the threshold of our entry door. Once inside, they drive us to distraction, chirping away in the early morning hours until, wild-haired and bleary-eyed, I find them, a shoe in hand. We ban our cat, Edgar, to the garage at night. He's not only as big of a pest as the crickets — wafting his tuna-scented breath in our faces and claiming badly needed bed space — but because he is also an avid cricket killer and gourmand. Personally, I can't think of many things more revolting to eat than a fat cricket; apparently it's an acquired taste.

The ivies are turning red, too. I like to see that, something as stealthy and unnoticeable as they are all summer, suddenly burst into flames of color as they slow their creep up the trunks of trees and fence posts in late August. I have seen a hint of yellow in our sycamores and tulip poplars and ash trees, as well, and the black walnuts are already dispensing with their green-hulled loads. The squirrels are reaping a near-record harvest this year, and I have skated on more and more of their fruitless shells as I attempt to negotiate our hillsides with a mower.

The first days of September also signal the end to the summer constellations. There won't be anything in the sky this month as bright as Jupiter, and already the massive planet and the moon are courting in the early morning sky.

We've begun to see the sun begin its twice-yearly run for the equator, depriving us a few minutes more of light each day. We have said goodbye to August's meteor showers and with them the warm night air will soon be gone. Not long ago, we saw the much-heralded "blue moon," which can be, among other things I am told, a second full moon inside of a month. We won't see another until 2015.

Everywhere I go, from the nooks and crannies of our back porch doorway to my barn loft to the dewy morning grass, I am finding more and more spider webs. I understand that the main reason for this, although I don't care for the whys when I've walked my big face through one, is that spiders sense the oncoming fall, so they expand their living quarters, get busier with mating, and store food. I imagine they'll be allied with the crickets soon in an instinctual Operation Overlord on my garage in the next few weeks.

I walked my walk each evening last week, and I noted that this summer's weeds are tired and haggard, that the corn is already rattling, and that nearly every butterfly I spotted had worn its wings ragged with its daily routine. The goldfinches have begun to peck away at the seed heads of our sunflowers, coneflowers and daisies, the drooped and faded gold and pink petals just another sign that a new season is coming along soon. Warm southern winds and toasted grass may be with us on and off through October; that is not unusual. But, it has not been a good summer for grasshoppers and tree frogs and honeybees, and the signs of change are undeniable, so be done with it.

There; I guess, this story wasn't so much work after all.

The Golden Rods of September

The sunflowers that are framed in my cabin's eastside window are soon to become things of the past, for no matter how much I water and weed, the time has come for them to go.

Just this evening, I walked around the back corner of the place and surprised a goldfinch tugging at a seed from a big yellow head like a dentist extracting a stubborn tooth. I suppose that little bit of a bird has grown tired of the thistle seed I keep in a feeder for him and his band of brothers, and I imagine he'll not rest until he pulls that first great prize from the sunflower, in turn beginning a general erosion of the whole thing.

The whirling blades of a ceiling fan are turning overhead, and I'm keeping a wary eye watching and hearing a sudden, gusty thunderstorm making its way across the soybean and corn fields to our west. We need the water, of course, and if I am to believe the weatherman, which I sometimes do, we are to get a little of it as a cold front blows in from parts north and cools us off in the days just before you are to read this.

In this reverie in the hours I have after work and before supper and bed, I am also re-reading a favorite book by Hal

19

Borland. Better known, I suppose, for his fiction, Borland also wrote what he called "nature editorials" for the *New York Times* for 30 years.

They are tiny gems of three or four paragraphs apiece, and they make me envious of his talent for putting pen to paper, and for seeing and hearing things I don't. A collection of the stories, ***Sundial of the Seasons,*** is my treat of choice right now.

An almanac of sorts, Borland's book spends a little time on each day of the year, and for my trip through it, I opened to the first of September with the intention of reading myself through to the end and back past the middle, a day at a time until next August. They are a devotional of sorts.

I, of course, have not made it very far at such an early point in the month, but his entry for Sept. 8 — my grandfather's birthday — was simply called "Goldenrod Yellow." In the span of just a few sentences, Borland gave me a lesson on the "weed" we've come to dread for its pollen and its contribution to the "hay fever" and sinus miseries that many of us endure. I didn't know, however, that goldenrod comes from a big family, one whose scientific name (*Solidago*) means "to strengthen" in Latin. It earned the name for its medicinal powers, and just as I read that phrase, I recalled a folklorist family friend who tried to desensitize my sister's miserable allergy woes decades ago by having her breathe a bit of smoldering goldenrod from a bag. I can't recall now whether it worked or not ...

Borland wrote: "Roadsides and meadow margins glow with the yellow plumes, and on a sunny afternoon the bees are almost as loud as they were at the height of clover bloom. Goldenrod provides a September harvest that adds a special tang to autumn honey. If it weren't for the goldenrod and the asters, which are rich in nectar, the bees would soon be out of business for the season."

September is a golden month, and I don't mean that only in the sense that we consider it a part of autumn, because technically, very little of it is. But it does serve as a signpost to the fall, and already I am seeing that proven true. The goldenrod is flowering in abundance these days; our ditches and fencerows are brimming with it. The soybean fields, too, are well on their way to turning to bronze, but first they spend a few weeks in a golden yellow stage, the dry fall days and cooler nights transforming them nearly unnoticed. There are now leaves of gold hanging on the dying stalks of corn, too; I noticed them yesterday on a walk, but also saw that the drying husks are opening their mouths to show off toothy hybrid smiles.

My sunflowers are, of course, a golden yellow, their faces turned to the sun nearly from birth. I don't know what variety I have growing in my garden; I never paid a bit of attention to the seed package we bought at the hardware store, not even to the planting instructions. Why, even a gardening nitwit like me would have to work to kill sunflowers once they've come up.

Sunflowers put off abundant pollen — like that goldenrod we don't plant and tend to — regardless of whether they are "Sunbrights" or "Autumn Beauties," "Velvet Reds" or "Italian Whites." I am told that the time to cut their heads is when the back of the flower has turned brown, but I don't think my flowers will ever face decapitation by pocketknife. My goldfinch buddy appears to have sent out a newsletter advertising my garden spot.

Years ago, as I rode by bicycle across the bubbling tar of the road on which we lived, I noticed a weed in the ditches that resembled the giant sunflowers that my grandfather grew in his garden. I didn't know it then, but they were "sunchoke," a bland Midwestern name for the Jerusalem artichoke, a plant that was cultivated by Native Americans and pioneers, alike. Unlike sunflowers, sunchoke was grown for its edible roots. I've read that it is now considered an invasive plant, for it is a tough old bird to kill off once it gets settled in, and I should know because I have a healthy stand of it growing along the fence behind my barn.

As I look out that aforementioned window, I can see that many of my sunflowers have been broken in mid-stalk, the birds and the wind riding them to the ground. I will have to pull them soon, but not today. Today is a day to look for gold, in the chrysanthemums I have blooming near my door, in the yardstick-tall coleus we've grown in an old wine barrel near our storage shed, in the early turning tulip-shaped leaves of our poplars. Toward the evening, it's my hope that this faux rainstorm will cede itself to a few rays of golden but fading sunlight, and it in turn will hand the sky over to a nearly full golden orb of a moon.

The storm is, for the most part, over now. It was mostly just noise and breeze, a few anemic drops of rain spotting the dust on my sidewalk. The only good thing out of it that I saw as I stood in the doorway eating an apple was the shower of golden black walnut leaves that had been caught in the pull of the wind and sprinkled atop my grass as if dropped from a sieve.

That old granite poet Robert Frost once wrote that "Nothing gold can stay ..." I understand that, so I had better enjoy it while I can.

The Magic of a Firefly Evening

I saw a firefly one day last week as I headed to our back porch door, my lunch already waiting for me at the kitchen table.

It was cool and sunny, and although it is not unusual for me to turn the blind corner from deck to door to find a wasp or spider or the flash of the skink who likes my flower bed sandstone, I was surprised a bit to see the lightning bug there in the middle of the day.

He, or she, was furiously motoring across my path,

laboring to get out of the way, so I stood and watched and waited as it crossed my street.

Fireflies are not quick, as far as the insect world goes — one reason they are prime targets for bats and dragonflies and humans. This particular bug reminded me of the ultra-light airplane that I sometimes see over my place — actually, a big kite with a motor and single seat. It seems to move very slowly across the horizon, buzzing and poking along just a few hundred feet off the ground. I think its pilot has plenty of time to take in the view from such a lofty and slow-moving perch, for he can see me waving from my yard.

I can't help but think that children are still amazed by the silent fireworks that lightning bugs put on for us in the summer, or at least would be if they spent more time outdoors.

I lived outside as much as I could when I was a boy, so along with an abundance of welts from mosquito and chigger bites and sandbur stickers, I came to know a little about fireflies, and still wholeheartedly recommend that we — even adults — spend a little time watching their bioluminescent gab sessions.

My less-than-scientific study of fireflies all those years ago helped me discover that it was on the most humid nights that I most saw them, and I also learned that keeping a few in a canning jar was fun for only a short while. If I wanted them to live, I knew I needed to enjoy their company temporarily or not at all.

That is how they entertain me yet today, often in those few minutes I hesitate at the door when coming to the house after my yard work is done, or I've worked into dusk at my cabin desk.

How unfortunate that so many children now, particularly those who really don't experience much summer darkness because of street lamps and city lights, can't enjoy the simple joy of fireflies in a meadow or roadside ditch. It might be just an opinion, but I feel that the glow from these wonderful creatures trumps that of a video screen or television, if just for a few minutes.

Science has gone to great lengths to discover how and why fireflies do what they do, but I still consider them magicians of sort. So does a friend of mine, Dr. Allen Young, curator emeritus of invertebrate zoology at the Milwaukee Public Museum. In fact, a chapter in his fascinating book, ***Small Creatures and Ordinary Places*** (University of Wisconsin Press, 2000), is called "Firefly Magic." In it, Young tells us just about everything we could possibly want to know about lightning bugs, including the fact that they aren't flies or bugs; they're beetles: "...harmless, soft-bodied, slow-flying ones called 'Lampyridae,' a word derived from the Greek and meaning 'lamp fire.'"

From reading just his single chapter, I have discovered that firefly larvae are called "glowworms," that they eat even tinier insects, such as mites and minute snails, that they aren't mature come fall, so they spend the winter under logs and tree stumps and rocks, and that a dry winter can lead to lower populations in the spring.

I learned that firefly flashing is primarily about sex, that it is the male that turns on most of the light to attract females, and that he is willing and able to emit 500 flashes and travel over a half-mile in a single evening to find the girl of his dreams. In a typical place rife with fireflies, males may outnumber females 50-to-1, so the former is most responsible for what we see come dusk. I had no idea when I was a kid what amorous and lurid scenes I was watching.

Young has taught me that there are many species of lightning bugs (about 2,000 in four large groupings); a typical one is Photinus, which he spent hours observing in a meadow. He said that mating usually lasts less than six minutes, and the mated female returns to her burrow as quickly as she can afterward, for she has only about 150 eggs ("low by insect standards"). If she dies before laying those eggs, the damage to the local numbers is considerable.

I watched fireflies through the magnifying glass of youth, used to sit and observe them as they silently moved about the horsetails and stagnant water of a marshy spot near our house a half-century ago. I knew that a firefly's light is a "cold light"; I couldn't get my fingers burned by handling them. Unlike the light that comes from a household bulb, which gives off only 10 percent of its energy as light, the lightning bug's battery and bulb — located in its body's last three segments — uses 100 percent of its energy for light. They do it by combining three substances in their "light organ." Two of them are "luciferin" and "luciferase," which got their names from Lucifer, the "bearer of light." When mixed with something called ATP, the firefly produces light, and does so in a series of Morse code-like impulses that only they truly understand.

"I was always fascinated with fireflies, even as a young child growing up in Westchester County, in New York," Allen recently told me. That affection is still evident in what he writes, and in his warnings to us, too.

"If we continue to exert pressure on nature's food chains," he writes in his book, "we will surely douse the lights of fireflies altogether, and our own well-being as a species will become a bit more tattered, a lot less rich." Young doesn't mean that inquisitive kids with canning jars are reducing firefly populations drastically, although they should get out of the habit of trying to keep them past a moment or two in hands and on arms. He reminds us of something we already know: Humans are destructive — often unintentionally — to the creatures that live around us.

"The great beauty of a summer night is born in the rot of these places (ditches and creeks), but it has to be pure rot, not the stuff of natural decay adulterated with the contaminating wastes of people. Compressing and poisoning natural areas surely douses the lights of a firefly evening, muffles the whispers of katydids and crickets, and does much more damage. ..." He adds, "I feel a touch of melancholy, a sense of loss that our children are not growing up with the wonder of fireflies and may soon know this feisty little beetle only through stories."

I think we are reminded a bit too often about the magic of our own doing, of the technology we have created for ourselves to teach and inform and entertain. Every so often, we need to be reminded the very best things in life are free, like a few minutes spent watching the fireflies in the warm summer air.

The Girl Who Wasn't My Grandmother

I have tried to picture in my head a funeral procession of black, spindly-legged Model Ts making their way across icy rural roads. It is a gray afternoon in March 1926. From the parlor of a small clapboard house in Brazil to an isolated and quiet Owen County graveyard, a grim hearse led the crawling procession east across the Old National Road to Manhattan, then southeast into the hilly countryside toward Fertig Cemetery.

Foremost among the mourners was my Grandfather Roy, for it was his wife, Beulah Jane, who had died; she was just 18 and pregnant, and they had been married less than two years. After that day, he would rarely speak of her again, and by doing so, he created a mystery for my daughter, Ellen, and me all these years later. ...

I'm not sure why Beulah's story has interested me enough to go in search of her. After all, she was not my grandmother, who was nearly worshiped in our family before she died at age 60. My grandfather married Blanche Nicely about a year and a half after his young first wife died, so any memory of Beulah faded away into the past, year by year. The little that anyone knew, or cared to share, about her eventually died with my grandfather, and my dad and my aunt. Years later, not long after my mother had passed, I found a photo in a basket of old snapshots she had kept in a closet. And in sepia tones of brown and yellow, there was my grandfather as he stood with Beulah, both smiling, both impossibly young.

"Who's that?" I asked my brother, John, for no one else was alive who could possibly tell me. "That was Pa's first wife," he said. "She died young."

Until then, I had never known there had ever been anyone in my grandfather's life before my grandmother, and I suppose that is typical, for we don't see our parents and grandparents as having lives, or being human, much before we are around to know them.

Years later, as I digitized old family photos so that my brother, sister, son, and his genealogy-obsessed older sister all could have copies, I kept coming across that same snapshot, wondering just who Beulah was, from where she came and where she was buried. A few weeks ago, I finally decided to try to find out.

The little that I knew about Beulah came from a story John told me. He said he remembered a drive that he, my mom, dad, and grandfather had taken one Sunday afternoon not long after my grandmother's death. He thought I may have been along for the ride, too, which makes sense, but I certainly couldn't recall it.

"We were all crammed into that old blue Buick we had," John said. "And I remember that we drove south of Manhattan, across John Grey Road (one of my grandfather's sisters, Alice, lived there), and we went through a covered bridge, and Pa kept saying that it was so icy the day of the funeral and the cars could hardly make it up 'Jackie Dunn Hill.'" He also said that my grandfather had gotten confused, and turned around as they searched for the graveyard, and that they ended up in several cemeteries, one that had a "white building near it." He wasn't certain that they had even seen Beulah's grave that day.

With those few clues, I picked up Ellen on a steamy Monday morning in July and headed to Brazil, where, like two rookie history detectives, we started our quest in the Clay County Courthouse. My grandfather's family, like many other large and laboring families of the day, moved where there was work to be found. Born in Parke County, he lived in Vermillion, Clay, and Putnam, counties, before returning to Rosedale in Parke, then eventually settling in northern Vigo County a few miles away. Born in 1902, he had at least 10 brothers and sisters, one of whom is buried in Missouri, and one who was killed at Haguenau and buried in France in 1945.

Helped by a kind lady in the county clerk's office — who upon discovering that I was going to write about Beulah in the newspaper, politely refused to give her name — we first found my grandfather and grandmother's marriage license application and license. The person who recorded the information listed Roy's occupation as "miner," and that it was his second marriage, his first ending in "Death." Erroneously, it was recorded that his first wife had died in 1924, and that error, and others on her death certificate, would soon prove troublesome.

It is an interesting thing to be amid the musty and yellowing records of a county courthouse. The rush of forced air, the rustling of old paper, and the quiet scribbling of another family's researcher excited us as we turned page after page and saw year after year of documents in hopes of finding what we needed. From the clerk's stash of records, we then were directed to the county health department, near the hospital, to locate Beulah's death certificate.

Ellen and I entrusted our search there into the capable hands of Lori Conrad, who claimed that she probably couldn't help me as much as a colleague, who was at lunch.

Yet, in just a few minutes (we first looked in the records for 1924), she led us to another yard-tall stack of registers, and eventually to Beulah's death certificate.

That thin strip of information yielded important data: Beulah had died in her home along East Jackson Street in Brazil on March 4; she had been born on Dec. 1, 1907, in Putnam County, and her father's name was Curtis Craft. Her attending physician was Dr. G.W. Finley; she had died of complications from nephritis, including "uremic eclampsia." In layman's terms, her kidneys quit working, and in those days before antibiotics, and because she was pregnant, Beulah couldn't fight her own body's toxins. Her blood pressure would have soared; she would have suffered convulsions; she probably would have slipped into a coma.

The death certificate went on to list a local funeral home as handling the burial arrangements and that she was buried in "Fertic" Cemetery in Putnam County. A quick search online showed us more than 100 cemeteries in Putnam County, none even close to that name.

Perhaps the cemetery had been renamed; perhaps it was so small or so isolated that few people alive could even tell us where it was. After placing a call to the Putnam County Health Department in hopes of getting cemetery records, and waiting a while in a local coffee shop for a reply, Ellen and I headed to Manhattan in search of a covered bridge, a long, tall hill, and a cemetery that held the grave of the girl who never became my grandmother.

Searching for Beulah Jane

The cicadas were singing in typical Hoosier summer refrains as my daughter, Ellen, and I stood waist-deep in the sweaty itch of a Putnam County cemetery's orchard grass and sumac. We were searching for the grave of my grandfather's first wife, Beulah Jane Lunsford, who died in 1926.

We had already had a long day when we found that tiny burial ground two weeks ago. With little more than the name "Fertic" and the faint recollections of a trip my brother took with my grandfather decades ago, the two of us were trying to get some closure to a quest that had started that morning in the quiet of the Clay County Clerk's office. We wanted to carve a small notch in our family's genealogical tree and along the way discover as much as we could about this girl who died at 18 and remains with us only through a single, faded photograph.

We arrived at the cemetery in a roundabout way. A dozen fruitless Internet searches and blank GPS screens behind us, we were awaiting a call from the Putnam County Health Office as to a possible location.

Rather than sit still, we were using some of John's misty memories as coordinates of sorts, so I turned south off U.S. 40 in the quiet little burg of Manhattan. I had visited my grandfather's sister, Alice Allen, and her husband, Everett, there many times, going to their farm on John Grey Road to camp and fish on Deer Creek. The roads, no longer bearing the names of people or geographics, were now numbered and impersonal. Yet, we found the Allen place, then drove on across Interstate 70, all the while rubbernecking for even a glimpse of a churchyard or family graveyard. Miles later, already frustrated from dead ends, roundabouts, and a maze of 425s and 1100s, we arrived back in Manhattan somewhat hopeless. Our long-awaited return call confirmed that there was no Fertic Cemetery in the county, but that it was possible that not all of the county's graveyards had even been mapped and marked. It was also possible that Beulah didn't even have a headstone.

We found hope at Krambo's Kustom Kolors, a busy motorcycle shop in Manhattan, its sliver of white rock serving as a temporary home base. Beth Broadstreet, who covers the counter at the shop, must have taken pity on me as I warily eyed the chops of the rather large bulldog that watched me when I walked through the door. She immediately tried to help by taking me across the street to a man often called the "Mayor of Manhattan"; the mayor was out. Beth then called Gerald "Mac" McClure, a retired county highway employee, who sent us southward into the country again, where, eventually, and in agreement with my brother's memories, we found a covered bridge, a long, winding hill and a cemetery located not far behind a small, white house. We thought we had found Beulah, too, but we hadn't.

The graveyard we searched was actually Matkins Cemetery. We got to it by wandering down a lane to the home of Joe Fox, just in time to catch him and his wife near their barn, moving horses from one pasture to another. Joe said he knew there was a cemetery on the back of his property, told us we could park in his yard, then volunteered to take us through a few gates into the woods. As we waited near a small concrete bridge that spanned a mushy ditch, we spotted Joe's work cap bobbing through the weeds as he poked around for a way to the graves. Forty-five minutes later, leery that we'd caught poison ivy, and scratching a few fresh mosquito bites, we were back in Joe's yard, he on the phone to his father, then his grandmother, then a good friend. We soon had directions south, then east, to Salem Cemetery. Despite some speculation that Beulah may have been buried with the Allens (that cemetery had an Allen plot), we came up empty-handed again.

Using the GPS, we now headed north, thinking that perhaps the covered bridge we had found on a map near the Boone-Hutcheson Cemetery, on the other side of Manhattan, was the marker John had in his head. We found the graveyard easily enough; it was perched high upon a steep hill, the view of the bridge and the cornfields below through the neatly trimmed headstones a beautiful one. Ten minutes after leaving that graveyard, which holds Moses Boone, son of the famous Squire Boone Jr. and nephew of the famous pioneer Daniel Boone, we literally stumbled upon the Manhattan Cemetery, unmarked on our map. We walked it stone by stone for most of an hour; there were Allens buried there, too, but no Lunsfords. Nearly 9 o'clock by then, a bit shy of patience and light, we decided to head home.

A break came later that night. Restless and unwilling to go to bed, I found the cemetery listed on a website. Working on the premise that perhaps the name had been misspelled in 1926, I discovered a "Ferdig" Cemetery in northern Owen County, a stone's throw from where we had been wandering. Beulah's death certificate confirmed that she had been born in Owen County. Within minutes, I had the coordinates and driving instructions, so the next day I called my brother and daughter, and we made plans to take another drive.

My wife joined us for the trip across curving Indiana 42 toward Poland. Convinced that I had accurate directions to literally drive to the cemetery gates, we headed north out of town on County Road 850E only to discover that there was no cemetery nearby. Several dry runs up field roads and long driveways got us nowhere, and once again I relied on the kindness of strangers, this time coming in the form of Doug and Beverly Rolison. I had hoped we hadn't interrupted the Rolisons' supper when I pulled into their drive. Eager to help us, they first explained that we weren't even in Owen County, we were in Clay, although both told me that I was within a quarter of a mile of where I could stand in any or all of three counties.

Doug said he knew of one graveyard nearby; he'd hunted near the property. So, he and Beverly jumped into their car and led us to it, or rather a place where, if I wanted to wield a machete and wear a pith helmet, I could have gone. Doug said he didn't think the graveyard had been mowed for 40 years.

By the time we left the Rolisons in a cloud of road dust, Ellen had the GPS locked onto the coordinates I had written down. It took us just 20 more minutes, and Ferdig Cemetery appeared around the bend in a gravel road — Ferdig Road — and we knew then that we could find Beulah.

She was buried near her parents, two infant brothers, and a sister. Her father, Curtis, had outlived everyone in his family by nearly 40 years. Nancy, his wife, had died in 1918 — the year Spanish Influenza killed a half-million Americans — when she was 35 and Beulah was just 11. Two of their children, the first born in 1909 and unnamed, the other born in 1913 and named Robert E., lived just two days. Another grave, that for Elsie, 1919-1921, goes unexplained, unless Curtis remarried.

In the wooded peace of that place, we could hear only the sweet calls of an Eastern Phoebe that sat on a wild grapevine near the cemetery fence. Beulah's gray granite gravestone marked an end to our search, and it is doubtful that we'll ever know any more about her. We stayed a while, recalling stories about my grandfather and wandering among the markers for familiar names. We went home north through Manhattan and Brazil, my grandfather's old haunts.

As we drove, I asked my brother about a brittle newspaper clipping I had found among photos at my mother's; my great-grandmother Clara must have kept it. It described a fistfight that my grandfather had been in while working on a road construction job south of Greencastle.

Apparently, Grandpa Roy, who couldn't have been out of his teens, took the worst of the fight, but both he and his opponent were fired from their jobs by the crew boss. According to the article, my grandfather's "older brother," James, who also worked on the job, then tracked down the other boy and gave him a "sound thrashing." Both he and my grandfather were fined.

We never knew my grandfather had a brother named James. Ellen piped in that there was a brother named Lee, too. We thought we had met all of Grandpa Roy's brothers and sisters, besides Hazel, who died very young, and Albert, who died in the war. Neither James nor Lee had ever been mentioned. Who were they? Where were they?

The search goes on …

The Beauty and Spirit of a Lonely Bridge

It was the best kind of day a few Saturdays ago: not quite 70 degrees, a slight breeze from the northwest barely pushed flat-bottomed white clouds around in an otherwise blue sky.

It was a day to sleep, until morning sunlight filtered through the blinds; one for spreading the newspaper out on the kitchen table and for drinking a few extra cups of coffee. It was a day with work to be done both inside and out, and one that supplied the time in which to do it. Straw and pumpkins and mums are selling at roadside stands now, and I have already been to the orchard twice to buy apples and take in the sweet air of the place.

Our asters and fall phlox are supplying purples and lavenders to the landscape, and we noticed on that perfect day of ours that the once-tiny woodpeckers in training that we've watched at our feeder — hatched in midsummer — are nearly as big as the red-headed father who spoon-fed them just a few weeks ago.

We are hopeful for a long and soft fall — one that goes on until we're happy to hand it over to Thanksgiving. So is a farmer neighbor of ours; it looks as though he'll get yet another cutting from his alfalfa field. Woolly worms are out and about now, too.

On that day, we spied two bright white worms that folklorists say are sure signs of heavy winter snowfalls. But, on other days, we've seen more light brown worms

than any other color; a few have even been coal black. ...
But that is a story saved for another day.

As we put shoe rubber to the road that evening, my
wife and I also noticed a few cars idling by us with
unrecognizable license plates and filled back seats. As
surely as fall has arrived, the Covered Bridge Festival can't
be far behind.

Our county, normally a quiet, thinly populated patch of
winding back roads, cornfields, and small burgs, attracts
visitors like moths to lamplight this time of year. It is a
disruption to the peace we normally have here, but one that
is necessary for the money it injects into the rural veins of
our economy. I often wish the festival was like it used to
be, smaller and as original as the hand-made wooden toys a
friend of mine makes in his shop to sell in town.

I used to wonder what attracted all of these people to
our county, why they'd fight the traffic and the crowds and
the lines at the port-a-potties. They leave towns and air
conditioning and online shopping behind to become
inspectors of hedge apples and examiners of weeds, and
they find awe at the sight of wooden gates and fading
barns.

I don't wonder about that anymore, and haven't for a
long time. Catching sight of the Harry Evans Bridge as I
drove around a bend on a dusty gravel road a few days ago
reminded me why I changed my mind.

On occasion, years ago, when the weather grew hot

and open windows and busy fans couldn't get us cool, we'd head to the creeks to wade and swim. My grandmother, who could see well out of only one eye, would load us into her blue Chevy Biscayne, aim it down the road as best she could, and drive us four or five miles north, down into Coxville, across Big Raccoon Creek and the Roseville Bridge, then north a bit more to the Harry Evans Bridge, where we'd spend an afternoon wading and sitting in the shallow stream it spanned.

As far as Parke County covered bridges go, it is small. Built in 1908, Harry Evans is only 65 feet long (by comparison, its neighbor to the south in Coxville measures 263 feet), a single pair of wonderful Burr arches (named for Theodore Burr, who came up with the idea in 1804) bending to support it as it crosses Rock Run Creek, which, in turn, feeds into the Big Raccoon a few hundred yards away. At one time, Rock Run was called Iron Run, no doubt for its then-reddish water, run-off from the many coal mines that operated nearby more than a century ago.

Of course, we didn't care about the particulars of the bridge as we played near it. We never thought about how it stood lonely on a lightly traveled road — that is until the festival came along. Because of its isolation, the bridge became known as "Kissin' Bridge," and over the years, it has survived arson fire and too-heavy trucks and annual floodwaters to sit as pretty as a postcard until we remember to appreciate it each fall.

According to Stan Sinclair, who wrote and illustrated the definitive book on Parke County's treasures, *The Illustrated Guide to Parke County Covered Bridges*, there was some dispute over naming the bridge after local landowner Harry Evans. Sinclair tells readers in his book that a man of that name lived in a place on up the gravel road and owned the surrounding land, but that at least one other neighbor took offense nonetheless.

My wife had her own Harry Evans story to tell. She used to visit an old man by that name when her dad made television repair calls. Living just a house or two north of Coxville, almost directly across the Big Raccoon from the bridge that carried his name, Joanie said he lived alone in a rambling dark old place and didn't seem particularly fond of children. "But that was my perception as a little girl," she adds. "He sure liked my dad, though; he kept his television going."

I sat on the stoop near our door and watched the sun say goodbye to that perfect Saturday. A little striped skink slipped out from under our woodpile and darted by my feet in a flash of blue and green. I was happy I had no cat on my lap to take interest in it. It had been a good day; a day that despite our investment in hard work and light sweat, we loved for its beauty and spirit.

We can easily understand why so many visitors drive our roads in the fall, stretching necks and pointing fingers and breathing deeply. We did just about the same thing when we came upon a green-sided covered bridge in the mountains of Vermont just this summer.

But, that's another story for another day, too.

"Everything She Did In Her Time Here, She Did With Love"

The last time I spoke with Sarah Norton, she was sitting at her office desk, leaning in a chair toward the light of the window.

She was my school's new assistant principal, and she was proud of it. After all, she had invested a lot of summer hours and late nights into earning an administrative degree, and for Sarah, time seemed to be more important than it is to most of us.

"How's it going, Boss?" I asked her as I poked my head through the doorway. I didn't call her by that name because she had taken on airs, but because she'd earned it. "I'm not your boss," she said, with a tired, beautiful grin. "You've been here too long to have a boss."

Sarah was gone from school the next day, and a few short weeks after that, she died of cancer. She was 31 years old. In the time since she passed, many of us who knew her, including those who loved her as daughter and friend, as wife and mother, as teaching colleague or student, have tried, without much success, to make sense of her death. But since we can't really do that, it seems easier to remember the impact she had on us with the too-short life she was given.

Sarah's cancer was cruel; it lied to her time and time again. It hit her several years ago like a freight train, then yielded a while to surgery, then came back, yielded again to chemotherapy and radiation, then came back again. Then it was more surgery and chemo again, but the cancer came sneaking back too.

Pink became an unofficial school color for us at Riverton Parke; the teams she helped coach wore it, her friends and relatives walked and raced in it; virtually everyone she knew believed in it, and they believed in her.

But the cancer didn't give up either, and each time it returned, it took a little more from her, until there just wasn't much more left to give.

Kyle Kersey, our principal, also in his first year at that job, saw how badly Sarah wanted to be an administrator herself, a school leader.

"Is it possible to truly define the 'it factor'? Well, I don't know, but I'm confident that Sarah had it," Kersey said. "Her leadership and work ethic and overall character separated her from the rest of the field."

Those of us on staff noticed that too. When we were certain that we couldn't possibly see Sarah at school after she'd looked so weary, so drawn, so worn down the day before, she would be there anyway, often sitting in a chair in the corner of a classroom, smiling, listening, nodding in that pink ball cap of hers.

"Very few things are ever given to people," Kersey added. "If you are the type of person that aspires to become a leader, you have to be a student first, let your heart lead you, don't be afraid to get dirty, and get to work. Sarah did those, and that is why she was able to accomplish as many wonderful things as she did in a very short amount of time."

Jackie Baxter knew Sarah as a teacher but loved her as a dear best friend.

"Sarah's most outstanding quality was the way she cared for others," Jackie said. "Last spring, she told me the news that the cancer was back, and she constantly assured me that it would be okay and comforted me. She was facing brain surgery the next morning, having just found out about it less than 24 hours before it would take place, and she was the one trying to comfort me.

"Her concern starting that conversation was that she did not want me to have to cry alone, and she was the one who was up against an obstacle that was so huge the next day. Whenever I asked her what I could do to help, her answer was always the same: 'Keep people calm and positive.'"

Jackie said, "I remember when a classmate passed away in high school, and it was almost as if he had instantaneously been named a saint. I didn't like that. He was my friend; he was a real person, and people have flaws and make mistakes, and sometimes those are great moments too.

"Sarah and I vented to each other about the things through our work day that pushed us to the edge, knew each other's order at fast food places for food runs between school and games, and while we ended up as mini-marathon finishers, it was neither pretty nor fast when we started and couldn't make it through one mile. ...

"She was the Thelma to my Louise, the Wilma Flintstone to my Betty Rubble, the Lillian to my Annie (that one's from *Bridesmaids*). We all know those shows just wouldn't be as fun without both girls in them. With just one, it's not the same."

Kori Wood knew Sarah as both a basketball coach and teacher; she is a sophomore at Purdue University now.

"I can only remember one instance when I was mad at her," Kori said. "She was running the free throw drill we did regularly at basketball practice that included a punishment based on how many baskets we missed. It just so happened that day I did a terrible job, which resulted in my doing 60 'burpees.' So as I was completing those, I silently blamed her for being so unfair, knowing the entire time it was really my fault."

"That was the thing about Mrs. Norton," Kori added. "You could never be mad at her. Her heart was too big, and her smile too warm, for anyone to feel anything but love when they were around her. That's what I will always remember about her, that everything she did in her time here, she did it with love."

Kids learn all kinds of lessons in school, and they aren't all in history and physics, algebra or English. Sometimes the learning comes from a lesson plan that is hard to understand. Sarah's life offered one of those lessons.

Besides the love of her husband, Dane, and her two young sons, Gabe and Gavin, and the rest of her family, I believe that lesson motivated her to keep trying, to keep living.

She knew that it wasn't just about the time she spent in the classroom or on the gym floor, or even behind that nearly empty office desk of hers. It was about the time she gave, willingly and without regrets.

Sarah understood the greatest truth there is in education: Teachers teach more by what they are than by what they say.

Poland Chapel Rises from the Ashes

I wrote a story a few years ago about how I came from a small rural community, how I was proud of the fact that I grew up feeling perfectly safe riding my bike into town, and how much I enjoyed wandering through Morgan's Variety or exploring the creaky old elevator in Rosedale.

I also mentioned how sad, and how afraid I was that the place, as I remembered it anyway, was nearly gone.

Along with a litany of reminiscences about drinking cold Orange Crush and getting flat-top haircuts and eating the ancient, hard rock candy I bought at a dark, old Main Street store owned by a woman who still wore button-up shoes, I mentioned that those particular memories had been incited by a deliveryman who had pulled up to my house with a pair of mail-order pants under his arm.

He told me that he was from Poland (Indiana's, not eastern Europe's), and he bemoaned that his hometown — and perhaps mine — were suffering a sort of creeping decline that was hard to watch. He wondered if in a few more years, memories would be all we would have of such places.

He asked me if I had ever been to Poland, and I told him no, that I had heard of it but had never driven through it. He told me not to blink if I ever did go, then he was off to hand packaged pants to other people.

Visiting Poland came back to mind last fall when Joyce Smidley emailed to ask if I'd be interested in being the second writer to come to that small community as part of the Poland Chapel Speaker's Series. Being a natural-born big mouth, I readily agreed.

So last month, I loaded up my books, polished my shoes and headed off through the country to find the place, which isn't far from the Clay-Owen county line. And, in it, as in my own town, I discovered that although it may be a little less vigorous than in decades past, it still has a story.

After meeting Joyce, and a host of others at the chapel, I felt a little more hopeful, too.

Had I never sold a book, or even been run out of town by bored listeners, the trip to Poland would have still been worth it.

There was a hint of autumn in the air on that sunny Sunday afternoon. The soybean fields were already turning to gold, and we heard the rattle of drying corn stalks moving in the breeze as we slowed for the hairpin curves and rollercoaster humps of Indiana state highway 42.

Poland straddles that narrow pavement like a saddle, but by the time we had reached the town, Joanie and I had so thoroughly enjoyed the drive that had taken us across the old Eel River Bridge and past family farms and neatly clipped lawns that we took in a little of the town, too.

We are in the habit of arriving early when going to unfamiliar places, so we did no more than idle past the beautiful white chapel on our way to a four-way stoplight. We decided to see the sights, and first took in the Poland Grocery and Hardware, one of those wonderful old amalgamations that become necessary for burgs that are just far enough from larger towns to make drives there inconvenient.

I tend to like stores where I can purchase toothpaste and copper tubing in the same place, so Joanie and I spoke to the cashier for a few minutes, bought bottled water and borrowed the restroom. We spied the "Cook's Corner" restaurant, too, and a post office, for Poland touts its own ZIP code.

By the time we got back to the church, which isn't far, Joyce — the chapel board's president — and her husband, Steve, had the doors open and a book table set up on the front lawn. Within 20 minutes, the church was pretty well filled with people, Joanie and I were introduced, and we settled in for an hour or so of storytelling. We were made to feel right at home.

I have wondered in the days since we went to Poland, in the years, actually, since my hometown began to fade, what keeps people in small familiar places when so many others are willing to pick up, pack up, and take off.

Joyce and Steve, and the folks who keep their eyes on and their hours invested in the old chapel, have stayed put, have kept the faith in Poland's simplicity and quiet.

"This historical structure," Joyce says of the chapel, built in 1869, then re-furbished in 2009 after arsonists set fire to it, "can never be replicated, and it is important to retain items and structures that tell the story of locations throughout our state. [The chapel] is a focal point of many activities and memories, not only for the community, but for many who have moved all across the state," she added. The chapel remains open one Sunday a month, hosts a Christmas cantata, a community choir, and an Easter "Sunrise Service," too. Weddings can be booked, despite the building housing only its sanctuary.

Prior to the fire (extinguished by Poland Volunteer Fire Department members who arrived on the scene within six minutes of an alarm), the chapel was open 24 hours a day, seven days a week.

First a Presbyterian Church, its ownership was transferred in 1929 to those who managed the nearby cemetery. By 1966, a band of dedicated citizens took it upon themselves to donate funds and labor, and they restored the church. When Joyce moved near Poland in 1986, she thought the building was "wonderful, and was intrigued by its history and the people who had cared for it." It was Tom and Marsha West who got her involved.

Joyce became a volunteer, and then she replaced Evie Frank as the chapel board's secretary, and has been working on behalf of it ever since. Although the Speaker's Series was Joyce's idea (the board has gotten great corporate support), she was quick to tell me that, "There have been many who came before me who are fully responsible for the chapel being saved." I can attest to that.

On that day, alone, I saw the great work done by Michelle Neese and Joan Nees, and had I had the time, I could have learned a lot more by speaking with Betty Herbert or Gordon Spelbring; they know even more about the chapel and town history.

Joyce also mentioned the great support of Poland natives Carolyn and Dave Thomas, and said that Wilmadean Baker, a longtime board treasurer, "worked long and hard to keep the chapel alive."

Before we left that day — and I might add that we were reluctant to leave the peaceful green of the shade trees just behind the chapel — Joanie and I stood with a few of our new friends and enjoyed homemade ice cream, courtesy of Craig Nees and Lloyd Burns, who are members of the Zion United Church of Christ.

They had made enough for everyone who wanted it that afternoon, and by the time I got around to asking for a second helping, it was gone. I think it was the best ice cream of its kind I have ever had, although Craig and Lloyd didn't offer to share their "secret ingredient" with me.

Joyce tells me that she "has learned a lot as she has gotten to know the people" of her community. Poland may be small, but it's far from being just a memory.

What 'Mr Smith' Can Still Teach Our Children

I am happy to say that many of the people I once called my students are now my friends; we stay in touch, and it is one of the true blessings of being an "experienced" teacher to hear from them or run into them in a store or restaurant, or even teach their children.

My wife, an elementary school librarian and teacher, has already seen the grandchildren of some of our first students come to her libraries, and as they file in, I'm sure she wonders where the years have gone.

Because I teach high school, and see my students a bit later in their lives, I suppose that when a third generation reaches my classroom, I'll have to consider leaving it.

Over and over again, I hear my "kids" tell me that they are afraid of the directions their own children's educations are headed. For the most part, they like the schools their children are in, like the teachers and administrators — even admire them — for the work they are doing.

They are afraid that perhaps a day is soon coming when they'll have no idea how to help their sons or daughters with the "new math" or help them cope with the frustrations of standardized test weeks, or even understand the rapid changes that seem to have a grip on schools these days. Of course, their parents probably had the same kinds of worries.

I recently heard from Bill Umstetter, who substitute taught with me when I wasn't much older than my students. Bill has done all sorts of things with his life since those days, including taking on the role of minister and college professor. He teaches ninth grade English now, too, and, as do all teachers, Bill has opinions about the growing importance of testing and data in our children's educations.

"I think that some numbers help us quantify situations, but others have no greater purpose than bureaucratic intrusion," he says. "When classrooms are mainstreamed, as they are in my district, data can be used to achieve any end, like blaming bad numbers on teachers or administrators, or they use good numbers as though the test brought them about. Common Core will drive the numbers game exponentially."

Although I feel testing and data gathering and number crunching have their places in education, I have never hidden the fact that in order of importance, they are fairly low on my ideal list of priorities.

Regardless of what we may think, we cannot measure learning with a test, and if we could, that measurement surely comes years after students leave the classroom. No test is perfect enough to do it, no column of numbers informative enough to show how and what a student feels or sees.

Writing assessment graders aren't intuitive enough to know just how far a student writer has come over the course of a year based on a student's essay response on a standardized test; they are grading that student at that point in time.

No set of classroom numbers can show a teacher's passion or desire, and grading schools and evaluating teachers based on testing alone is ridiculous.

Am I saying that data collection and standardized tests have no place in schools? Of course not. My generation — whose education was driven by a space race and the threat of nuclear war and the Iowa Basic Skills Test — grew quite used to its own "new math" and "student tracking," and a whole host of other trends, some of which are still with us, others that have fallen by the wayside.

Regardless of what we want to believe, we have used children as educational lab rats over the years; we did it with "Touch Math" and "Open Concept" schools, and a litany of "new ideas," some of which worked, and some that didn't. We should keep trying, and it's important that our children see us trying.

But, ultimately, statistics are not going to prove whether we have done a good job of educating our kids. The teachers I know are not resistant to change; change makes our worlds go 'round. But we want meaningful change.

Although she was at one time a proponent of President Bush's "No Child Left Behind" movement and had great faith in the results of testing and assessment, Diane Ravitch is now considered a traitor by many of those who know just how much she thinks the whole thing was a mistake.

"Education is not about amassing data. Education is about changing the lives of students; enabling them to become wiser, more thoughtful, more intelligent, more judicious, and to grow in health and character," Ravitch wrote in her well-read blog two summers ago.

I also heard from one of those "former" students a few days ago. Heath Rohr is a sophomore at the Air Force Academy in Colorado Springs, Colo. Heath was a serious student in high school (I'll forget about his drowsiness in my last block class every other day), and remains a serious student now. He has to be that at the Academy, or he'll be shown the bomb bay door.

Heath dropped a message to me last week to tell me he'd just watched the Frank Capra classic, *Mr. Smith Goes to Washington*." We didn't watch the film in any of the courses he'd taken with me, but we had seen a healthy dose of Capra in my Film Literature class a few years ago; I now show "Mr. Smith" in my Mass Media course.

Heath admires Capra's belief in the common sense of the "little guy," and he understands that Capra elevates honesty and courage and citizenship to a level of greatness not seen in modern films. More important, Heath understood why I bothered to show his class a few films that were made well before his grandparents were born, and, heaven forbid, are in black and white.

When I think of "Mr. Smith," one scene comes to mind before all others. In it, Jimmy Stewart's Jefferson Smith, the patriotic and idealistic everyman who has filibustered against the corruption of a cadre of senators and publishers until his legs can no longer hold him, looks up from a basket of fraudulent telegrams. Although exhaustion and sweat are etching pain on his face, he meets the eyes of the unnamed and sympathetic President of the Senate (played by Harry Carey). The latter's smile, his faith in and sympathy for Smith, teaches viewers a lesson in kindness and compassion that can't be measured by a test, but certainly needs to be taught in schools, as surely as algebra and verb conjugation and the periodic table of elements.

Teachers understand that businesses need qualified workers, that minimum standards need to be taught, that tests need to be given and data compiled. But above all, teachers need to be helping young people become decent human beings who do the right things, who work hard and keep trying, and who realize that their education is just beginning by the time they take the "End-of-Course Assessment," not ending with it.

Thankfully, I teach at a place where I can still show my students what Mr. Smith can teach them. I hope that never changes.

Suckers for a Good Pumpkin Sale

My wife and I are fairly frugal; we are budgeters and planners. In the fall, we set aside what we'll need to heat the house and pay the doctor and buy sensible shoes for school. I think we're going to have to open an account for pumpkins, too.

I know, that's an exaggeration — writers are known to do that — but we do spend a lot of money on pumpkins each fall. We love them, not because we are just avid carvers of jack-o'-lanterns and makers of pies, but because we admire their colors and shapes and sizes. Visitors to our place will find pumpkins near our doorways, on my cabin porch, adorning the straw and mums under our poplar tree, and sitting near the cedar archway we have in the front yard. We buy them at roadside stands, grocery stores, and hardware centers. We're just suckers for a good pumpkin sale. ...

Pumpkins are, essentially, the final fruits (somewhat of a biblical term; they are actually vegetables) of the year, so tossing them over the back hill in the waning days of fall for the deer to eat means winter can't be too far away. We have had rogue pumpkins grow wild on our hillsides where the shrunken heads of old jack-o'-lanterns and their decorative mates have been disposed of the fall before.

But I have never felt I've had the proper amounts of sun or garden space to try to grow them myself. As a result, we get our pumpkin fix off local dealers; I'm sure they're glad to see us coming.

Pumpkins are actually squash (I thought they were gourds, but they all come from the same family, as do zucchini). They contain healthy amounts of lutein and alpha and beta carotene, and are great sources of vitamin A (essential for our eyes and immune systems). I remind myself of how good they are for me while I eat the pumpkin pies my wife so graciously and expertly provides to our household. I am always certain to apply vitamin-enriched whipped cream to each slice as well.

Although pumpkins are grown all over the world, they are native to North America; seeds have been found in Mexico that date back some 9,000 years, and the first

Europeans to get lost, then find their way here, discovered pumpkins already being cultivated and eaten. Pumpkins get their name from the Greek, "pepon," which means "large melon." The French adapted the word to "pompon," and from there the British referred to them as "pumpion." Colonists took it a step further and began to refer to them as pumpkins.

Pumpkins are, of course, commercially grown, and Indiana is amidst a belt of states that leads the nation in their production. After pie-baking, the most obvious use for them this time of year is for the carving of jack-o'-lanterns, something my sister and I used to co-op with my mom at the kitchen table years ago. With a layer of newspapers laid down to catch the mess, my mom, wielding a butcher knife as expertly as Mother Bates, would get the proceedings under way by sawing out the top of the pumpkin for us.

My daughter and son (and now daughter-in-law, a carving rookie who found "gutting" a pumpkin repulsive until she joined our clan) carry the tradition onward, often laboring away on October Sunday nights after a big dinner has been cleared from our old oak table. My wife adds to the occasion by roasting and salting the pumpkin seeds afterward, a treat that my daughter stuffs into the side of her face like the late Tug McGraw's chaw.

Jack-o'-lanterns, like many other customary trappings associated with Halloween, have an interesting origin. The dictionary — usually my favorite resource — gave me virtually nothing on them, so I turned to a number of websites, including that of the History Channel, to get my information on the tradition. The story most often repeated about the origins of the decoration comes from Ireland with the tale of "Stingy Jack."

It's told that Jack was so cheap that after he invited the devil to have a drink with him, he refused to pay the tab. Instead, he convinced Old Scratch to turn himself into a coin to pay for the drinks, then pocketed the money, keeping it next to a silver cross to hold the devil at bay. Jack eventually let the devil go in exchange for keeping his soul out of hell, then tricked him again for another 10-year delay from the fiery furnaces. When Jack did die, he obviously was unfit for heaven, but the devil wanted no part of him, either, instead opting to leave Jack to roam the earth with nothing but a lighted coal to show the way. Jack placed the coal in a carved turnip, and thus the jack-o'-lantern was born. The Irish, then the Scotch, made it traditional to carve frightening faces into turnips and potatoes to scare old Jack away from their doorsteps. The custom came to America in a wave of immigration, and has been with us ever since.

Although jack-o'-lantern carving has become a bit more sedate of an activity at our house than it was years ago, it has also become more artistic. Daughter Ellen now goes to great length to buy extravagant patterns for her carvings, starting her career with rather uncomplicated cats and bats, then progressing to spider webs and ghosts. This year, she's opting to sculpt Vincent Price.

We had tree trimmers at our place last week, and their bucket truck and chipper were parked in our narrow drive the same morning my wife had to back out of the garage and get on her way to the store. Not wanting to get too close to the equipment, she accidentally backed over two large pumpkins we had sitting along a flower bed. When she pulled forward, she couldn't have flattened them any better had she dropped them from a parking garage roof.

It didn't really matter that much; we had more than enough money left in the pumpkin budget to replace them. In fact, I think she bought another half a dozen.

Inching on Toward a Cold Winter

I'm not ready for snow and ice and the daggers of a north wind, but I have finally accepted the fact that winter is nearly here.

For that reason, I was in my barn one day last week, shelving a few flower pots that I had just extricated from the clutches of the frost-bitten petunias that were soon to join faded friends on the compost pile.

I had to move a bale of straw to get to one of the shelves, and as I hiked it on top of another nearby, I noticed five or six black-and-brown wooly worms curled up in the vacated space.

We don't keep as much straw as we used to, not even

bothering with tossing it into the loft anymore. We no longer have a horse, as we did when we first moved to our place, and our kids gave up rabbits long ago. I keep the bales handy for the occasional lawn seeding or for a place on which to sit pumpkins and Indian corn for fall decorations, and a little more for sprucing up a winter box for our old cat, Max.

I was more than content that the worms found a warm place to bed down until spring, and I don't intend to move the straw again until I get back out into the yard come March.

We have seen a bumper crop of woolies this fall, peak season coming about a month ago, as Joanie and I still walked in shirt sleeves and in warm sunshine with a bit of wind.

But like a former friend giving us the cold shoulder, the weather has turned on us now, and since the clocks have betrayed us as well, we walk in darkness and cold more often than not. Even the wooly worms have enough sense to avoid doing that.

By the time I made a return trip to the barn, this time with a rake and a shovel I'd used in transplanting a few mums from plastic to earth, I noticed the worms were gone, inched off, I suppose, to another secret spot, probably just a bale or two away. They are welcome to stay as long as they want.

Had I paid much attention to the worms, they might

have been able to — at least according to the old-timers I know — tell me what kind of weather we are going to have this winter. No, I don't store a bottle of corn liquor in the barn with my tools; they don't actually speak to me.

I would have simply checked to see how black the worms were, for it is commonly believed that the more black bands on the worms, the more snow and cold weather we'll see.

I have always tended to hedge my bets on the side of science when it comes to weather predictions. Besides, I can't say that I have seen any hornets' nests this fall to test another popular cold weather theory, nor have I cut into any persimmons to assay yet another. But I have always believed that science can fit hand-in-glove with some folklore, so as far as wooly worms go, I've gone in search of answers.

The worm in question is actually a wooly bear caterpillar (also called a "back-ended bear"). As the larval form of *Pyrrharctia isabella* (the Isabella tiger moth), we see them most often in mid-fall after they have left their food supply — typically dandelions, nettles and plantain — to search for cozy, dark spots to sleep for the winter. Those beds may come in the form of leaves or mulch, tree bark or a seam under a rock, and in my caterpillars' case, between two bales of straw next to a grumpy old cat's bed.

The wooly bear — "wooly worm" is considered a term that originated in the southern part of the country — has 13 distinct segments. In fact, folklorists claim those segments match perfectly with the 13 weeks of the winter season, and that the larvae can "tell us" whether we'll have early cold weather or whether we had better keep the snow shovels handy for those near-springtime blizzards.

Some believers claim that even the directions we see the worms headed in late fall are predictors: If they are headed north to south, you'd better lay an extra blanket on the bed; they're fleeing cold arctic air.

Another popular wooly bear theory is based on the "wooliness" of the larvae's "coats." If it is particularly thick, that, too, is an indicator of a cold, cold winter. Short of keeping last year's caterpillars in the freezer, I'm not quite sure how we're supposed to know the current crop is sporting heavier-than-usual coats though.

Rather than simply speculate, I went to a scientist to get an opinion; National Oceanic and Atmospheric Administration weather forecaster Jeff Boyne obliged.

"I am not sure whether I would consider myself as an expert on the subject," Boyne said. "I just kept hearing about this over the years and wanted to write something about it. Some weather folklore does have some scientific basis to it, but this one just does not have any scientific fact. From what I have read about the woolly bear, much of the colorations that we are seeing are related to different species or age. Some species will turn more brown as they grow."

A study done in 1948 by C.H. Curran, Ph.D., curator of insects at the American Museum of Natural History in New York, pretty well backs Boyne's science. Curran collected wooly bears for eight years, carefully measuring and weighing and observing them, and his conclusions were about the same: Caterpillars really don't predict much of anything.

It's most interesting to me to know that the black-and-brown caterpillars that are sleeping amidst the dust and rust of my barn will be moths next spring. As far as moths go, the Isabella tiger moth is not particularly large or colorful. They'll wake up when the weather begins to warm a bit, spin peach-fuzzed cocoons and, a few weeks later, enter adulthood like we all eventually have to do.

My wife told me the other morning, as I walked my unshaven face and tossed salad hair past her to the bathroom, that she was happy that she hadn't had to wake me up the night before to catch a snake that had found its way from our garage into the hallway. She scooped the little guy up — a frightened garter just looking for a dark, warm place to snooze — and deposited him in the woods.

"I heard that finding snakes in the late fall is supposed to be a sign of a warm winter," she told me.

Here I go again …

"I'm going simply because I've got to ..."

Late in the year 1944, the great Hoosier war correspondent, Ernie Pyle, mentally and physically exhausted from his months reporting from the battlefields of Europe, came home for the last time. He was scrawny and gray.

"I am leaving [the war] for just one reason ... because I have just got to stop," he confided to his readers. "I have had all I can take for a while."

A few months later, already restless with four walls around him, Pyle decided to return to the front. Reporting the war from the Pacific, he landed with the Marines at Okinawa.

"I'm going simply because there's a war on and I'm part of it, and I've known all the time I was going back. I'm going simply because I've got to — and I hate it," he wrote. On April 18, 1945, Pyle was killed by a Japanese sniper's bullet on Ie Shima Island. In his pocket was the draft for a column he intended to complete when the war was finally over.

"In the joyousness of high spirits," Pyle mused, "it is easy for us to forget the dead. Those who are gone would not wish themselves to be the millstones of gloom around our necks. But there are many of the living who have burned into their brains forever the unnatural sight of cold dead men scattered across the hillsides and in the ditches along the rows of hedge throughout the world. Dead men by mass production — in one country after another — month after month and year after year. ..."

I have thought about Pyle's words these past few days before today — Veterans Day — arrived on my doorstep. I have never fought in anything bloodier than a grade school recess scrap, have never worn a uniform, was happy that I had to worry only a short time while my Marine Corps nephew served a brief stretch in Iraq. Like many of us, I suppose, I have been buffered from the real fear of war, and I know that I can't possibly understand those who wake up to it every morning and go to sleep with it every night.

That wasn't so of my great-grandparents, Jim and Clara Lunsford. They had a large brood — 10 children — that came in two volumes, the first that included my grandfather, and a second that brought my still-living great uncle, Tom, over a dozen years later.

They said goodbyes to four of their sons, Will and Bob and Albert and Tom, as the boys left fresh-faced for military service during World War II, and in one tragic case, never saw one of them again. Albert, a private in the 314th Infantry, 79th Division, died near Hagenau, France, on Jan. 23, 1945; he wasn't yet 26. Jim and Clara were told that he had been killed by a bomb from a German jet-propelled airplane, and that he was buried in the military cemetery near Epinal.

Albert is still there, in the foothills of the Vosges Mountains with 5,254 others; his grave is marked by a white marble cross; his serial number was 37744181.

On the night before he was killed, Albert wrote his last letter home. Ironically, he mentioned in that note that he had been able to see his brother, Bob, and that he was happy that they had been able to spend a night and a day together. Bob wrote a few lines in the letter, too.

I found Albert's picture in a book that commemorates the servicemen of Parke County; he is listed among the surprisingly large number of "Gold Star Boys" who also died for their country. I studied the photo a good while, and although I know I couldn't have met him, I see that same face in my cousin, Gene, Albert's son, who came to live with my grandfather and grandmother after his dad was killed. I see that face in Gene's children, too.

Ernie Pyle was right when he wrote in those final notes, "To you at home they [the dead] are columns of figures, or he is a near one who went away and just didn't come back."

Today, I'll remember Albert. He is buried in France, in B Plot, Row 17, Grave 20.

"The Mind Is a Dark Forest"

If you hadn't noticed by reading the newspaper or hearing me crow about it myself, I have another collection of stories out in print. And over the past few weeks, I've been out and about peddling them with the heart and soul of a hungry Fuller Brush Man. It has been a joy to see old friends who have bought the first three books I've compiled; it's been a real challenge to remember their names, too...

The whole scenario reminds me — if I remember correctly — of a cartoon by the late great Jeff MacNelly. His Pulitzer Prize-winning "Shoe" was one of my favorite strips, and in one, the irascible columnist, Professor Cosmo Fishhawk, stares at his overflowing, impossibly crammed desk and says, "I don't get it. ... I can remember every word to 'This Ol' Heart of Mine' by the Isley Brothers. But I can't remember where I put my stapler. ..." As he continues to stare, he mutters, "The mind is a dark forest."

Amen to that! It seems as if the more I try to stuff into this wrinkling cranium of mine, the more that falls out when I'm not looking. Names, it appears, seem to be dropping like flies.

A great example of that problem presented itself just a few weeks ago. I was merrily signing books at Baesler's Market (I can still recall the chilly wind wafting up my pants leg as we sat near the front doors), and Dick Becker, who I've met a half-dozen times around town, and who owns personally-signed copies of my first three books, approached the table.

He must have seen the look of utter confusion on my face when he began speaking to me, for I was carrying on a completely different conversation in my head while he spoke, a tiny voice imploring the name-recalling lobe of my mushy gray matter to kick-start itself. I finally admitted to Dick that I had forgotten his name, and being the gracious fellow that he is, he told me not to worry about it. "You meet a lot of people," he added.

Convinced that the bit of forgetfulness was temporary, I greeted a number of other readers, drank a cup of caffeine and ate an apple fritter. I nearly choked on the latter when Mel Gastineau came around the corner. "I know this man," I began to think to myself, but I also knew I'd remember his name 10 minutes after he left.

"I hate to tell you this," I told Mel, "but I can't remember your name," my pen poised to scribble his name. Mel, like Dick, was gracious. "Don't worry about it, Mike; you have a lot to remember," he said.

Like Cosmo, I don't get it, either. I can remember Carl Yastrzemski's batting average from 1967, the year he won the Triple Crown. I can remember I got a C in Algebra I my freshman year from Mr. Norris, and knew even then that it was a gift. I can remember the phone number of my seventh-grade girlfriend. I can remember that my step-grandfather wore a Bulova wristwatch, and I can vividly recall the few seconds of puckered revulsion I had when I ran my tongue across a piece of alum I found at my grandmother's house, believing it was rock salt. I can remember the names of most of the students I had in my first year of teaching, even where they sat in my classroom.

But, I couldn't recall the names of two men, both of whom I had seen over the past few months.

I had my picture taken with Mel when I spoke at the retired Vigo County teacher's luncheon last summer, for gosh sakes ...

Do I have too much aluminum in my diet? Should I start drinking filtered water and sprinkling blueberries on my cereal? Do I need to work even more crossword puzzles? Take up Sudoku? Get to a memory clinic? Probably not ...

I asked someone who should know. Dr. Paul Reber, an expert in brain, behavior, and cognition at Northwestern University, and director of the prestigious Reber Lab, which studies the "cognitive neuroscience of learning and memory," tells me I shouldn't get too concerned, yet.

"The key piece of why names, in particular, are hard," Reber tells me, "is that they are completely arbitrary. Other facts or general pieces of information connect better to other things we know and things that 'hang together' are remembered better. Seemingly random numbers, like batting averages, have meaning — how much better or worse was that average than the players' previous years? League/team averages? Tell somebody who isn't a baseball fan some batting averages, and they won't remember them."

Reber added, "But names are arbitrary and so they are hard. As we age (Reber is 46), our memories all gradually get a little worse at learning new facts (remembering old facts stays about the same), and it's the hard things like names that we notice first."

The good doctor is a very busy man, but he also took the time to say, "I go to a lot of conferences, and I will frequently be approached by a student whom I recognize that I have spoken with before, but I have no idea what their name is. ... This will sometimes be disappointing to them because they hope I'll remember them. The thing is, I do remember them — I can generally tell them everything except their names. Why? Because all of that other information fits together and because it hangs together, pulling up some of it helps pull up the other related information. But not the name. Nothing about the rest of the information gives me any hint as to what their name should be."

He went on to tell me that unless I was having other neurological symptoms that are affecting my memory, I shouldn't be concerned at all.

So, this morning, after checking to be sure I had on the same two shoes and had recovered my ring of keys from the entry door where I had left them last night, I headed to work confident in the fact that I wouldn't get lost.

I also know that I have a pair of book signings coming up soon and that I'm going to have to look at least a few of those who come in right in the eye and tell them cheerfully, "I know your face, but refresh me with your name."

"God Bless Us, Every One..."

The year 1842 was supposed to be a triumphant one for the English novelist, Charles Dickens. Already hailed as one of literature's most popular figures before he was yet 30, the author of **Oliver Twist** and **The Pickwick Papers** arrived in the United States in late January to begin what would become a five-month stay in a country that he believed to be a true republic.

Dickens hoped to find democracy at work in a superior way to his Victorian England, which was at the time a sordid picture of class prejudice and misery for its working poor. At first, he found America all he had hoped it would be, but week by week, he came to dislike much about the place, ridiculing the corruption that riddled its government, irritated by a lack of international copyright laws that took money from his pockets, even criticizing American table manners, or rather what he saw as the lack of them.

After a week in the nation's capital, Dickens was convinced that America "was not the republic of my imagination," and later wrote in his travelogue, **American Notes**, which he published in October, that Washington was rife with "Despicable trickery at elections; under-handed tamperings with public officers; and cowardly attacks upon opponents, with scurrilous newspapers for shields, and hired pens for daggers." It was as he also said, a "headquarters of tobacco-tinctured saliva."

Despite being genuinely impressed that he was able to

go anywhere he wished and see anything he wanted to see, and that America was a place where true democracy was trickling down to the masses, Dickens could not tolerate the existence of American slavery, and his critical *Notes* led him to a falling out with readers and politicians and friends in the States, including Washington Irving. His next major novel, ***Martin Chuzzlewit***, was also critical of Americans.

Dickens had exhibited a bit of the reformer's zeal and optimism in his early work, but after his tour of the United States, and subsequent trips in early 1843 to the tin mines at Cornish, where he saw wretched working conditions for children, and the Field Lane Ragged School, which was established to help educate the homeless and starving street waifs of London, the author's work began to turn darker, his concern for the poor greater.

Already fueled by the unforgettable experience at age 12 of working in a blacking (shoe polish) factory while his father served a term in Marshalsea debtors' prison in 1824, a tribulation that stayed with him his entire life, Dickens undertook to write ***A Christmas Carol*** in September 1843.

Subtitled "A Ghost Story for Christmas," the book also took on the conditions of England's poor, and, in doing so, became an instant success.

Dickens' dedication page read: "I HAVE endeavoured in this Ghostly little book, to raise the Ghost of an Idea, which shall not put my readers out of humour with themselves, with each other, with the season, or with me.

May it haunt their houses pleasantly."

I have been re-reading Dickens' "Ghost of an Idea," these past few days; it won't take long, for it is just 86 pages. Despite a furnace that works well, old Ebeneezer Scrooge's chilly counting house, and even colder heart, keeps me from feeling cozy. Dickens describes him early in the book: "The cold within him froze his old features, nipped his pointed nose, shrivelled his cheek, stiffened his gait; made his eyes red, his thin lips blue; and spoke out shrewdly in his grating voice. A frosty rime was on his head, and on his eyebrows, and his wiry chin. He carried his own low temperature always about with him; he iced his office in the dog-days; and didn't thaw it one degree at Christmas."

Dickens penned *A Christmas Carol* at a time when England was in somewhat of a revival when it came to celebrating Christmas. Just two years before the book was published, Queen Victoria's German-born cousin and husband, Prince Albert, had introduced the "Tannenbaum," or Christmas tree to England. The British had begun a revival of singing Christmas carols, as well.

Why has Dickens' story persevered? I asked Dr. Matthew Brennan of Indiana State University's Department of English that question. Brennan teaches British Literature, and often includes Dicken's *A Tale of Two Cities* and *Bleak House* on his course syllabus.

"The story lasts, I think," he said, "because it is about

the possibility of redemption, a fitting Christmas and New Year's story. And it is about reclaiming one's lost best self, about connecting the past to the present with hope for the future. Its blatant sentimentality, though artfully presented, makes it appealing and popular, too. The season is a time of auld lang syne, and the 'Carol' exploits this nostalgia."

Brennan went on to explain that Dickens is often credited with creating our modern idea of Christmas, perhaps along with American Clement Moore's poem, "The Night Before Christmas" (which pre-dates Dickens' book). "Its very imagery resonates with our traditions. Dickens knew how to entertain readers as no one else in his time," Brennan added. "Maybe we like, too, how we hate Scrooge, but come to feel empathy for him as he joins the communal celebration."

There is little doubt with the year he had just put behind him that social criticism was on Dickens' mind during the fall he wrote the book. Like other Victorian writers (Brennan points out Carlyle, Ruskin, and Elizabeth Barrett Browning), Dickens was "deeply troubled by the dehumanization brought on by the Industrial Revolution. [Bob] Cratchit's near-poverty and its influence on Tiny Tim is central to the plot," Brennan adds.

Over the years, we may no longer see *A Christmas Carol* as the ghost story Dickens intended, nor as commentary on a system that preyed on children and the poor, as he also wanted it to show.

We choose instead to remember Marley's clanking chains and Tiny Tim's crutch, old Fezziwig's party or Scrooge as he huddled in a cemetery gazing at his own tombstone through tear-streaked eyes.

We recall Ebeneezer's "Bah, humbug" and Tim's "God bless us, every one," as well. We have adapted it to stage and screen and to comic books, have brought in Muppets, Scrooge McDuck, Mr. Magoo and George C. Scott to play the primary roles, and yet, Dickens' story remains, for the most part, as it was so many years ago. The book has never been out of print.

I hope to finish this little book one night soon when I can prop my feet against my fireplace's hearth, a place that reminds me of some of the evenings I spent in my parents' house.

And if it is true that we all take from Dickens our own favorite memory, then I have one, too: It comes when Scrooge is with the "Ghost of Christmas Present." They are watching Ebeneezer's niece and nephew, who, despite being adults, are playing games.

"For it is good to be children sometimes," Dickens wrote, "and never better than at Christmas, when its mighty Founder was a child himself."

Mike Lunsford

'Tis the Season for Sending Christmas Cards

This story is not a pathetic plea for mail; I get plenty — just ask my local recycling center. But it is that time of year when Christmas cards start showing up in my mailbox, and lest you think I equate those yearly offerings as junk or an annoyance, I have to tell you that I actually enjoy getting — and, yes, even sending — Christmas cards.

I am old enough to remember the Stone Age of the United States Postal Service; a time when emails and text messages and Facebook posts could do it no harm; when stamps needed licking and most people actually wrote something besides a hasty signature in their cards.

My mother used to pull her Christmas card list out of a beechwood desk in November. By the first week in December she was spending part of her mid-mornings at the kitchen table, writing long letter-like notes in dime store cards, almost always ones adorned with Wise Men who sat perched on the backs of camels, a single star lighting the blue eastern sky.

I guess Mom ruined me for Christmas cards. Although I value the friends and acquaintances who take the time and treasure to send cards — even electronic greetings — to us, I think I most appreciate those who write a paragraph or two in them, perhaps just to let us know they still can employ cursive or think a little without a computer spell checker. Those kinds of cards stay with me a while, and I still recall that even years after I left my parents' house to be married and take on home repairs and mortgage payments in earnest, my mom still sent cards to us. She lived three miles away, but she believed that a card said something special, particularly because she took the time to do it right.

Christmas cards that hold photocopied family letters are alright by me too. In fact, I write a letter to include in our cards, mainly because my handwriting is so terrible. I don't want recipients to think that I hastily scribbled a note to them without forethought or interest, so my letter is typewritten. Most of my friends already know that even if I hold my tongue just right I can't scrawl more than a few lines without some calligraphic disaster; yet, I still scratch a note in blotchy ink rather than have them feel I have mass produced my Christmas sentiments.

Family letter writing is an art. I can't imagine that any of us make it through every single letter we receive without scanning a bit to the end. Old friends may have just landed that big promotion or had a gallbladder removed, but we can be happy for their incomes and digestive tracts without having to read about them in extended detail. I prefer to hear a story, a "Remember when?" or "Can you recall?" that brings back warm memories, but truthfully, I'll even read about a balky gallbladder if that is all the writer has to offer.

Christmas cards have been around for ages, the tradition beginning in England in the 19th century. Wanting to know more about card customs, I contacted James Cooper, a UK native who loves everything about Christmas, including the sending of cards. In fact, he's an expert, and he founded whychristmas?.com, a website devoted solely to the traditions and foundations of Christmas.

Cooper tells me that the sending of cards can be traced back to the English in 1843; one Sir Henry Cole, a civil servant who had an interest in how common people used the "Public Post Office," got together with an artist friend — John Horsley — and designed the first Christmas cards, selling them for the equivalent of about a nickel. He made and sold about a thousand of them, and the very first card depicted three panels — two that show people caring for the poor, and a third that shows a family enjoying a Christmas meal. Those first cards could be mailed for about a penny. Cole's cards, and most of those Victorian Era cards afterward, did not have religious themes, but rather emphasized artwork and good wishes.

Within 20 years, the practice had really caught on; posting costs had been reduced to about a half-penny, and cards were not only being mass produced, but had taken on more religious significance. By 1900, sending Christmas cards had become extremely popular in Europe, particularly in Germany. As early as the 1870s, Christmas cards were catching on in the United States too, particularly those developed by German printer Louis Prang. By 1915, John C. Hall and his two brothers created Hallmark, the largest card-making company in the world, but despite that, Americans still spent much of their own time making and sending their own cards.

Cooper maintains that sending cards is more than mere tradition. "There's something much more personal about a real card, rather than an email, Facebook message, tweet, or SMS (Short Message Service). Someone has taken the time to get cards, write them, and put them in the post. It's probably the closest many of us get today of actually writing 'real letters,'" he says.

"I've got some books containing prints of old Victorian cards, and some of those are amazing. They were far more adventurous in their designs than we are today. They had cards with animals (dogs, cats, frogs, and bats were particular favorites), clowns, crosses decorated with flowers (more like Easter or 'with sympathy' cards we send today), and even scenes of summer and bunches of spring flowers, looking forward to the new year. I'd love to see more variety in the cards we have now," he added.

I learned from Cooper's webpage that as of just three Christmas seasons ago, Americans sent 1.5 billion Christmas cards, more than any other country in the world, and that the average U.S. citizen spends over $30 a year on cards.

Joanie and I will, of course, hold up our end of that bargain again this Christmas; we'll dutifully sit down in several kitchen table sessions (I have made a concession to address labels) and get our cards ready to go. Many of mine will undoubtedly be received after Christmas because I almost always wait too long to get started.

But we'll be sending them. After all, the Postal Service can use all the help we can give it.

The Times Were the Best Present Ever

I am writing this piece well before Christmas Eve, although you wouldn't think that it can be far away by the look of things out my windows tonight. The panes sport just a bit of frost in their corners as the mercury heads below zero, as we had been told it would, and an icing of new snow spreads out as far as my lamplight can reach. It's not that I don't have plenty to do: I haven't addressed a single Christmas card, nor wrapped one gift. It simply feels and smells and sounds like Christmas tonight.

Eyeing my own breath in the air as I walk between house and cabin step, catching the scent of fir from the wreath at the door, and hearing the familiar voices of Bing Crosby and Johnny Mathis coming from my stereo speakers have put me in the mood early. A cup of hot coffee and a place to prop my feet may just keep me in it for a while, too.

I have been trying to think of some story, dredge some

fragment of memory from Christmases-past for a column, but not much has come to mind these past few weeks. I asked my brother for help at our Thanksgiving table last month, knowing I'd be writing this for the day before the day before Christmas, and he deadpanned that he didn't really have that many fond memories of childhood Christmases. Then again, he is an occasional Grinch, but my sister stayed mum on the subject, too.

The manger scene my grandmother set up on an old living room coffee table each year came to my mind. It had a radiant blue Christmas tree bulb fixed under its eaves that served as a faux north star. It had apparently led the Three Wise Men to Baby Jesus' bedside, their faces frozen in a rictus of adoration.

The livestock looking on were a sad sight, for years of handling by six grandchildren had worn and chipped their paint. The Christ child lay swaddled in a bed of excelsior, everyone in the ensemble stilted and motionless. I used to sit in front of it, knowing that our gifts would be spread out around the table come Christmas Day. My grandmother, a deeply spiritual person, always reminded us that opening gifts should be done with the Savior in sight, and I can't remember too many times that she even made much of a fuss over a Christmas tree in her house.

My aunt's tree was an entirely different story. It was a rather spindly aluminum model, which could have easily doubled as a television antenna in the off season. It had a multi-colored wheel grinding away before it, casting the whole corner of her living room in a garish kaleidoscope of oranges and reds and blues. If I recall, she, too, had a manger scene on display at her place, but that tree, packed in its original box and brought up from the basement in the first week of December, was one Christmas tradition on which we always relied. I sure hope it was eventually recycled into a bass boat.

Most of the people who were in my grandmother's coal-fired "front room" — or my aunt's, for that matter — are gone now, the years getting away from those of us who still remember those days. We usually heard homegrown gospel music at my grandmother's house during the Christmas season, but at ours, we listened to the traditional classics from Bing and Gene Autry and Nat King Cole. As a matter of fact, we heard them just a little more than we really wanted to ...

I have related many Christmas memories through this space, so you may already have heard about our gas log and frozen front porch and the Noma bubble lights that fascinated me. I might have even related the time my aunt gave me a roll of rope as a Christmas gift and how I was scarred for life by the experience of choosing it to open one Christmas Eve, the only present we were allowed to even touch. But I haven't said much about the endless Christmas Eve nights my brother and sister and I spent together, often imprisoned in a single bedroom, my dad a Sgt. Shultz-like guard, stretched out on the couch.

After being sent to bed at what seemed to be about four in the afternoon, we were allowed to leave our dungeon only to use the restroom and get a drink of water, perhaps use the restroom again, then sip a bit more water, then, of course, use the bathroom. ... Each time, we hoped for a glance at the tree, and each time, we were told to get back to bed. Our only solace in our cell was the radio, one that glowed a pleasant orange and illuminated the three half-faces that huddled around it listening to an endless litany of classic Christmas songs until we drifted off to sleep. By the time midnight rolled around, even the announcer was reduced to simply telling his audience the time, which, of course, seemed to move in two- and three-minute increments.

I came to know the lyrics of many of those songs as I lay on my bunk, hands tucked behind my head like William Holden in *Stalag 17*. Of course, Crosby's "White Christmas" was probably the most-often played. All these years later, I find it hard to believe that Irving Berlin wrote that hopeful song while grieving; he and his wife regularly visited their son's grave on Christmas Day, for in 1928, the Berlins' three-week-old boy died on Dec. 25. We, of course, heard the song before and after Christmas; the movie *Holiday Inn* was almost always playing on the television.

I came to love the silky Nat King Cole's rendition of

"The Christmas Song," too. Mel Torme — the "Velvet Fog," "Mr. Butterscotch" — who I often heard on many a Sunday night variety show when I was a kid, wrote the song on a hot summer afternoon in 1944, hoping, he said, to cool himself off. Cole first made it popular in 1946.

"I'll Be Home for Christmas" was my favorite — still is — and I didn't care that it was Crosby who sang it, too. Written in 1943 by Kim Gannon and Walter Buck, it, of course, comes from the perspective of a soldier, stationed overseas, who wants to go home, a sentiment shared by many women and men in our military right now.

The more I've sat here, looking out to branches blowing in a stiff north breeze, the glow of a string of green-and-red lights at my eaves, I can still hear those times, those people: Judy Garland singing "Have Yourself a Merry Little Christmas," Rosemary Clooney vocalizing "Silent Night," the whiskered Burl Ives wanting us to have a "Holly Jolly Christmas" …

Those were good times, times that were the best present I could have ever had.

"Stille Nacht! Heil'ge Nacht"

By most accounts, Christmas Eve on the Western Front in 1914 was one of uncharacteristic quiet and peace. As a bright half-moon shone through a smattering of clouds, cold, still air froze the deep mud of "No Man's Land" with a covering of frost. The stars shone, although in places, a light snow fell onto the heavy wool coats of the soldiers.

Across the shell-torn landscape, the troops of the 'Fatherland' could be heard as they sang from their trenches, "Stille Nacht! Heil'ge Nacht, Alles schläft; einsam wacht…"

Private Albert Moren, of the Second Queens Regiment, remembered that "Silent Night" as he sat in the trenches across the killing zone: "I shall never forget it. It was one of the highlights of my life. I thought, what a beautiful tune."

Rifleman Graham Williams of the Fifth London Rifle Brigade recalled: "First the Germans would sing one of their carols, and then we would sing one of ours, until when we started up 'O Come, All Ye Faithful,' the Germans immediately joined in singing the same hymn to the Latin words, 'Adeste Fideles.' And I thought, well, this is really a most extraordinary thing — two nations both singing the same carol in the middle of a war."

The Great War had begun that August, two titanic armies colliding in the Low Countries, particularly in Belgium, where in and around the ancient city of Ypres, in Flanders, they had been deadlocked in a slaughterhouse of a struggle that began in October and, by the last day of November, had claimed a quarter-million lives; there would be two more major battles fought in the area in the years to come, and they would be even worse.

By December 1914, the trenches of the two armies stretched from the English Channel — not that far from Ypres — nearly to the Mediterranean Sea. Neither side's governments showed any inclination toward entering into peace talks.

Yet on that night, and for the first and only time in the war, peace came to at least small portions of the front in what was soon to be called "The Christmas Truce." Today is the 100th anniversary of that Christmas Day observance. The combatants — Scots and Saxons, Englishmen and Bavarians, Westphalians and Welsh — had not fought much past the usual sniping and shelling and trench raids since the 19th.

Instead, they had dug themselves in to wait for replacements and supplies, and in those six days before Christmas, nearly every man along the Ypres salient — on both sides of the fight — had received gifts from home. Those on the British side took joy in the special five-inch bronze tins they'd received. The tins, paid for by the Sailors and Soldiers Christmas Fund, organized by King George V's 17-year-old daughter, Princess Mary, held cigarettes and pipes, pencils and sweets.

Many German troops had received some of the nearly half-million fir trees that had been sent from home, and in many spots along the battle lines, those "Tannenbaums" were adorned with candles and placed on the parapets.

Yet these local "armistices" had been agreed upon primarily so both armies could bury their dead, and to prepare themselves to manufacture even more. According to most of the men who wrote letters home of the event, it was the Germans who had made the first move on Christmas Eve, and again the next day. Capt. Charles Stockwell, of the 2nd Welsh Fusilliers, claimed he heard at least one of the "Boche" clearly shout, "We don't want to fight today."

Within minutes, soldiers from both sides were meeting to trade tobacco and sausages, belt buckles, the precious contents of the Princess Mary tins, uniform buttons, and clothing. Addresses were exchanged, as was news, and it was agreed that there was to be no fighting the next day.

The Christmas truce held. Despite orders from various headquarters that the "fraternization" was forbidden, even officers took part in the impromptu meetings in the killing zones between trenches. Photographs were taken, some soldiers even wrote home of "football" games that were played (although that is debated to this day), and up and down the line the men of both armies sang Christmas carols, applauding the efforts of the other.

Second Lieutenant Bruce Bairnsfather, who survived the war to become famous for his drawings and cartoons, wrote of the truce, "It did not lessen our ardour or determination; but just put a little human punctuation mark in our lives of cold and humid hate."

Bairnsfather added, "This indescribable something in the air, this Peace and Goodwill feeling, surely will have some effect on the situation here today... There was not an atom of hate on either side that day; and yet, on our side, not for a moment was the will to war and the will to beat them relaxed."

Someone who knows as much about the truce and the war as anyone is Peter Simkins, who is nearing his 50th year as a professional military historian, the past dozen at the Centre of Excellence in War Studies at the University of Birmingham.

He told me that he felt the Christmas Truce "has been blown out of all proportion as an incident in the Great War. It was, to my mind, an interesting, localized, and brief incident, which proves neither one thing or another about society at the time."

"There are plenty of examples of unofficial and undeclared 'live and let live' scenarios in the rest of the war," Simkins said. "Saxon troops were notoriously unaggressive, given the chance, but it is equally easy to find examples of blood lust after a buddy was killed, and so on."

Captain Stockwell remembered the morning of December 26: "At 8:30, I fired three shots into the air and put up a flag with 'Merry Christmas' on it on the parapet. He [a German] put up a sheet with 'Thank You' on it, and the German captain appeared on the parapet. We both bowed and saluted and got down into our respective trenches, and he fired two shots into the air, and the war was on again."

Perhaps the event has been glorified, and when compared to the unprecedented butchery of the years to come in that war that was supposed to end all wars, it isn't that significant. But the Christmas Truce was not the first, and surely has not been the last instance when enemies put down their arms to meet in their own versions of "No Man's Land."

Let us hope it will not be the last.

A Whiner Speaks of Pain and Suffering

I have one eye closed as I type this story. If I force the other one open, I see two blurry, pink keyboards; two of everything, for all that matters.

As of yesterday, my yearly sinus infection — the one I'm sure that came straight out of Dante's *Inferno* — has come calling with all claws bared, and I'm just going to have to wait it out.

If it is true that virtually all colds and sinus infections get started after the victim comes in contact with any one of 200 different viruses, I believe I have met up with 184 of them, and they all are mugging me at once with the biological equivalents of brass knuckles and rib kicks. Just about every muscle in my body hurts, with the exception of my left pinky toe. My head feels like it's been stuffed with cotton, and I have a headache that makes a liar out of every ibuprofen commercial in the history of television sales pitches.

Of course, I'm to blame for much of this thing. When I first started feeling the aches and the sinus pressure, and experienced those first nagging little hacks and coughs that whisper — to sensible people — warnings of an oncoming illness, I ignored them and continued to go to ball games and work outside and visit with family and friends over the holidays.

Clearly half the people I've been in contact with were also trying to ignore their cold and flu symptoms, so while we were hugging and back-slapping and shaking hands, and handling the same serving dishes and breathing in the same polluted living room air, we were also sharing our nasty little viruses. I must say that I got a good one in the annual Christmas grab-bag this year.

I realize that a cold and a sinus infection and the flu are three very different animals, but when I get one, I tend to get at least one of the others. Sinus infections supposedly harass about 31 million Americans a year (a number I find low), lead to 16 million doctor visits, and are responsible for about $1 billion a year being spent in the process.

I know, I should be thankful that I can do my part for the American economy this week by buying tissues and cough syrup, by dripping on things and enduring chapped lips and a raw nose, but if my attempt to get a little sleep last night is any indication of what I am going to have to endure to do my bit, I'd just as soon go ahead and donate my body to science.

Of course, like any red-blooded American male — who usually has the common sense of a gerbil — I have been doing whatever I can to put off the inevitable trip to the doctor. Obviously, I don't want to sit in an overheated waiting room filled with other sick, wheezing people; I am thinking about investing in a hazmat suit if I finally have to go.

This morning, after a long night of attempting to rest in bed, then on the couch, then on the family room floor, and finally in an old recliner, I started the usual exploration of our medicine cabinet to see what I could take for immediate relief.

Like just about everyone else, I have managed to keep every medicine that I have taken since I had impetigo when I was five. I know I need to dispose of old nasal sprays and antacids, but I just never get around to it. I found one bottle of "expectorant" that was expired only by a month, so I'm pretty certain it's not going to kill me.

Of course, there are old-time remedies to consider. A cousin I saw recently at the petri dish we call a Christmas reunion told me she starts her fight against all colds and flu and sinus bugs by knocking back a good stiff shot of whiskey. But apparently it has done her no good; she also told me she was currently on three different kinds of prescription medications.

My own grandmother, as devout a person as I ever knew, and very much an anti-saloon leaguer and true hater of the evils of drink, often administered corn liquor for "medicinal purposes."

In the days before rural medicine reached the American West, I have heard that it was advised to eat a roasted mouse when coming down with a cold. Some old-timers even believed that catching fall leaves in your hand — straight from the tree, mind you — prevented illness all winter long; I'm too late to try that one.

Many old remedies involved sheep and cow dung, specifically teas made from them. One remedy for the flu — I'll probably get that, too — called for placing sulphur in the sufferer's shoes. Sore throats allegedly could be taken care of by taking a dose of fir tree turpentine that had been sweetened a bit with sugar. Obviously, none of these fixes appeals to me.

Years ago, the patent medicine industry included all kinds of great things in its cold, sinus, and flu remedies: cocaine, mercury, lead, and opium were very popular. For a while, medicines containing even radium and other radioactive materials were touted for a variety of illnesses, too.

So whether I drag myself to the doctor or not, I guess I'm lucky that if I have to feel crummy, I am at least doing it in a day and age where my prescription won't involve cleaning a barn stall or handling uranium.

But, I do plan to set a mouse trap in the garage tonight.

Seeing the Miraculousness of the Ordinary

It was just a few nights ago that I announced to my wife that I was headed outside to watch the International Space Station pass overhead. Despite our having finished an early supper, it was already dark, and a fresh north breeze had brought that day's unusual warmth to an end, the temperatures already down to the teens, the wind chills even lower. I grabbed a coat and scarf and gloves and left the house in a hurry, for the television weatherman had said just moments before that the treat would be short-lived.

I hadn't been outside long — just a minute or so — when I heard Joanie coming out the garage door to join me; she was already looking into an inky sky dotted with flickering stars, and Venus was showing off as usual to our southwest.

"Where do we need to look?" she asked, not knowing that I was smiling over the fact that she was beside me, as she most often is when I decide to walk out into the yard to see this or that. We are alike in that regard, easily entertained, country-raised, so birds at our feeder, a shooting star, a box turtle, or flock of geese are sights we enjoy.

"Well, unless I'm mistaken, it's right there," I said, pointing northwest toward what I understood to be the brightest thing we could have seen in our night sky just then.

Without a blink, the silver point of light — a few sets of solar panels reflecting the sun in a way we couldn't really understand since we stood in the dark miles below — moved steadily across the sky toward the eastern horizon. It took just long enough to leave us, traveling, I am told, at about five miles a second, to make my neck ache and my face red.

"Well, the show's over," I said after we took one more glance aloft and watched our breath create dewy clouds in the air.

Until today, I had forgotten that night, for its ordinariness comes from years of practicing similar things. But the memory of it came back to me at about the same time I remembered meeting Christine Clark a few weeks ago. She introduced herself — her son, David, too — as I sat tucked behind a table signing books and sipping coffee at the Coffee Grounds in Brazil. She also added, "I thought you might want to know that I lived a good while up on Tick Ridge."

Of course, I knew the place of which she spoke; it is, as the crow flies, no more than a mile or so from my house. There are other Tick Ridges, as remarkable as it seems; one is near Waynesboro, Pennsylvania, another in Washington County, Ohio, and yet another is in Carter County, Kentucky. But, since I have written about the Harry Evans

Bridge, which sits nearby, and of the time my dad ran his goat cart (you read that correctly) through a triangular-shaped patch of wild raspberry bushes on "Briar Hill" near there, she knew I knew where it was.

Christine is proof that sometimes stories walk in the door to greet me, for I was happy to hear of her days going to Coxville School and her memories of the huge pine tree that sat just outside her bedroom window, the sounds of the wind blowing through its needles still echoing in her head. She remembered how she and her friends relished a sip from a shared RC Cola, a bottle of which they bought because they could get more to drink for the money they pooled. She recalled how a friend, Rex Jukes, used to snatch buzzard eggs out of nests, and how he used to try to get his laying hens to hatch them. "He had a goose that chased cars, too," she added. "It was the funniest thing."

Christine also recalled the endless summer days when she and her friends played on the sandstone cliffs near Rock Run Creek, just north of her home in what was really just a little collection of clapboard houses in those days. Her father was a tenant farmer who made his home in a number of places, but above most memories, she remembered the Evanses and Jukeses and Virostkos who lived nearby, and the hard work and good times they shared together.

As much as I enjoyed hearing Christine's stories — similar to the ones told by parents and grandparents who grew up on similar ground — it was something else that she added, almost as an afterthought, that most stayed with me.

"We've taken the anticipation of joy away from our children," she said. "Why, we used to all run outside to see an airplane pass over our house, just so we would have something to do. Children have too much now, and they always seem bored."

She's right, of course. We do seem to grow easily tired with the usual things, with the familiar and simple these days, and I'm not speaking solely of children, either. But, this is not a tirade against the hand-held, not a rant against connectivity and convenience and social media, but rather a realization that I need to seek in this new year the remarkable in the commonplace, for beauty in the everyday.

The British poet, Andrew Motion, says we need to "honor the miraculousness of the ordinary." Christine Clark's stories reminded me of that a few weeks ago, and looking up to the stars one cold winter night proves it to be true.

The Encouragement of Compassion

I didn't know Braeden Hollowell, and I didn't know the two beautiful, young girls who died with him earlier this month. The automobile accident that took their lives has been inadequately called a tragedy. But what happened that day, and in the days that followed, goes beyond words.

To Braeden's parents, to his school, to his community, and to the hundreds, perhaps thousands, of others who came together to grieve, to remember, to console one another, I feel I need to say that you are a credit to the human race; you have done it the right way; you have proven that, once again, we can take comfort in the compassion and faith we have in us.

Braeden, just 17, and his best friend, Ethan Lee, 18, who survived the crash, were like brothers. After young lifetimes spent together, they had recently led their North Vermillion Falcons football team to a Class 1A Indiana State High School championship. Ethan spoke at his friend's funeral.

Sisters Annie and Caroline Clark, both of Muncie, attended Cowan High School; they were just 18 and 16. Their family is struggling with their losses, too, but still wanted to be at Braeden's funeral because his family needed them there.

In the days of shock, of final preparations, of the solemn yet wonderful tribute to Braeden at the school days ago, community response has been overwhelming. North Vermillion Principal Jayne Virostko, who once sat in my classroom as a student, says she can't describe what she's experienced at the school near Cayuga.

"I have so many stories of the compassion of people, and the support that has come from small schools and small towns where the people are family, not just people," Jayne told me.

I asked her to share a few of those stories with me, and she told me what Jeff Pope did. Jeff's association with the school is as a representative with Josten's, a national custom jewelry designer that creates, among other items, class rings.

Along with his brother, Jason, and father, Gordon, Jeff worked a long weekend to get a state championship ring made for Braeden's family to have. The three of them then traveled two hours to come to the visitation that Monday and told Jayne there was a chance the ring could be ready.

Because of severe weather, the overnight shipping truck was not going to make it in time, so Jeff contacted UPS, then drove to meet the truck a few hours away, making it back to the funeral service just seconds before it started.

The ring was handed off like a football from one person to the next until Jayne gave it to head coach Brian Crabtree and assistant Justin Fischer. They, in turn, gave it to Braeden's mom, who, along with her family, slipped it onto her son's finger. He was already wearing his state championship medal and game jersey.

Then, Jayne told me about Braeden's competition — the teams he played against. Many of them — entire teams — came to the visitation. Linton, Covington, Seeger, and South Vermillion attended the funeral, as did Rockville's team.

When the Miners, who the Falcons defeated in the regional round of the state tournament, walked into the gymnasium that night, Jayne said the place went as silent as a stone. They had driven nearly two hours, then stood in line for two hours more, their respect earning respect.

The next day, North Vermillion received a floral arrangement from Pioneer High School; the Panthers fell in the state championship game to the Falcons.

Of course, there have been stories about other kids, the ones who thought enough to dress in Falcon blue and white, even though they attend other schools, schools that are the rivals NV often faces on the basketball court, the football field, and the baseball diamond.

Even elementary school kids in the area donned the Falcons' colors. The vast majority of the students and teachers at our school — Riverton Parke — did it, too, and when our principal, Kyle Kersey, asked that we observe a moment of silence in remembrance of Braeden and Annie and Caroline, it was silent; it was reverent.

Braeden's death hits home with us; not long ago, many on the staff and in the student body at North Vermillion wore pink when our school family lost Sarah Norton, our assistant principal, to cancer.

Stories about the loss of young people like Braeden have been told too often, and every school, every community has its share of them; I know ours does. It has been 32 years this spring, when I was a young teacher and coach at Montezuma High School, that two of my students — Jamie Rumple and Harold Wittenmyer — were killed in a car accident as they returned to school from play practice.

Jamie and Harold were wonderful kids, and one of their best friends, Lisa Atkinson Kneeland, now a grade school teacher in our corporation, was involved in the accident with them. Lisa shared a story a few days after Braeden's funeral, recalling that not long after the accident, North Vermillion's drama club dedicated its performance of "Oklahoma" to the students at Montezuma, the little school just down the road and across the river.

Not much time goes by that I don't think of Jamie and Harold, and I know that is the case of so many others who knew them too. They will never be forgotten, and neither will Braeden and Annie and Caroline, and the precious handful of others whose faces never age past their last yearbook photos.

The word, "special," came up often when I heard stories describing Braeden, but one seemed to define him better than most. He once told his stepfather, Marty Brown, the athletic director at North Vermillion — a man who has been in Braeden's life since he was three or so — that he thought it was "weird" that he was getting awards and recognition for things he "was just supposed to do."

That lesson in humility was something that Braeden

not only learned, but also was something he must have taught, for so many others have come forward to do things in these difficult days without expecting anything in return. For instance, Jayne told me that the entire NV football team traveled to Muncie to attend the funeral service for the Clark sisters. It was just what they were supposed to do.

It is a belief as old as the Scriptures that we are to encourage one another, that we are to build each other up. That has been done in the face of unspeakable pain in times gone by. It is being done now.

The Night the Snow Fell

You would think that the cold winds and deep snows that we endured two weeks ago would be old news by now, but as I stood in the checkout line at a grocery store just a few days back, a gallon of milk in one hand and a quart of orange juice in the other, a customer just ahead of me appeared to be stocking up to make a run for the Donner Pass, and all she could talk about was the storm.

I've listened to numerous tales of hardship and depravation these past few days, at the bank, the local gas station, and at a hardware store, where I thumbed through a rack of insulated bibbed overalls, a pair of which I have every intention of owning before this winter is over.

There have been stories of dead car batteries, drifted roads and icy slide-offs, and one friend told me that a few rooms in his place registered 32 degrees after his overtaxed

Mike Lunsford

heating unit gave up in its effort to outrun the storm's fury. The "Polar Vortex" of 2014 has not only left a trail of burst water pipes, wheezing furnaces, and potholes in its wake, it has forced me to finally admit that I am no longer a big fan of winter. This has been a cold season, one that started well before the calendar told it to, one that seems to be about as welcome as uninvited relatives who have little intention of leaving anytime soon. No, this winter has already given me my fill of shoveling snow and cracking fingers and trying to keep my truck between the ditches.

I am, of course, more than old enough to easily recall the "Blizzard of '78," the measuring stick that everyone uses when bitter air comes sweeping down from Canada to smack us around. It was, in my humble opinion, a much tougher animal to deal with than this year's storm, despite the fact that there was nearly a 70-degree difference between the high temperature last Monday and the miserable Monday before. The storm of '78 lasted longer, dumped more snow and left us isolated here in the country, all cold hard facts that are more palatable now with the proliferation of four-wheel drives, cell phone communication, and back-up generators. That's not to say that I wasn't worried on the nights this storm's winds blew and its snow fell; I worried plenty.

Joanie and I tried to avoid the shark-infested waters of the supermarket the Saturday before the storm arrived. We got our cupboards stocked a few days earlier, topped off the tanks of our car and truck, made sure the barn cats (one, a big hungry freeloader that appeared on our step two days before the big blow, and who is available for adoption) had a good layer of straw to tuck around themselves, slipped an insulated cap over our outside faucet, changed our furnace filters and hunkered down in the house to wait for things to happen.

By the time the heaviest snow came — and kept on coming — I had brought wood into the garage if we needed to open our fireplace, and began the trek to our bird feeders, amazed from the very beginning that our feathered friends were managing to get to the supper table at all, considering the brutal winds that raked across our yard like backhanded slaps.

Luckily, we never lost power, and despite a worrisome, but temporarily frozen water line to our refrigerator's ice-maker, we came through the mess with little more than sore backs from shoveling and the creeping dread of a record-setting electricity bill coming in the mail.

In January 1978, I was doing my student teaching at a rural school just south of Crawfordsville, living in a rented apartment in the quiet little town of New Market. Because I was on a very limited budget — something between abject poverty and canned soup twice a day — I closed off all the rooms in my half of a duplex, using only the living room, kitchenette and ice cube of a bathroom. There was a certain Hefneresque feel to the place, since I had to set up my bed in the living room. Sleeping in the bedroom there would have required a ski mask and a sleeping bag suitable for Peary's assault on the Pole.

My time in New Market was a mixture of excitement and pure drudgery. Those were the days of long-distance calling, so I used to head to a mom-and-pop gas station/grocery along the main drag in town to call my then-girlfriend, who decided the next year to marry me. Commiserating with my situation, she had spent the previous winter — a terrible one, too — getting her student teaching done in Vincennes. She lived in a one-room upstairs apartment, where, minus a freezer, she kept her frozen pizzas on the roof.

I gained a certain confidence in being able to fend for myself that winter, while the kind old lady who lived next door kept me alive with generous care packages of freshly baked cookies. My teaching took a back seat to the 13 days of school we missed, so many days that I was told I had to live on in New Market a while longer, subsisting by then on a steady diet of cornbread that I baked in an old iron skillet (the mix was only about 12 cents a box) and shivering my way through snowy afternoons of watching Phil Donahue on my 14-inch television and reading Shakespeare.

One memory that will stay with me forever came after I dug my Plymouth out of a massive drift to drive — with the requisite 300 pounds of concrete blocks in the trunk — a few miles north into the country to eat supper with my cousin, Rick, and his family. Coming up over a rise on their narrow road, just a mile from the single flashing light in New Market, I met a National Guard tank as it cleared the road with an enormous blade.

The rumor is that the Vortex is to come calling yet again this winter. If it does, I'll continue prayers that my power stays on. I'll be willing to shut off rooms to conserve heat if I have to; I'll even eat a little cornbread for old times' sake.

The big advantage now is that I won't have to call my girlfriend long-distance.

To Sleep, Perchance to Dream

I've been thankful this winter for a full propane tank and ample cold cranking amps and school snow-delay days that have kept me off the roads until the sun is up on the most frigid of these mornings.

I've appreciated more than my fair share of beautiful winter sunrises and sunsets, too. Grumpy old January, now history, gave us dozens of calendar-worthy pictures of clouds and cardinals, hoary frosts and snowdrifts; February promises the same. And, while I am trying to remain positive about these shorter, darker days and bitter temperatures, I have to say that this winter has also reintroduced me to the joys of sleeping well.

Never a prodigious sleeper, as so many of my high school-aged students claim to be, I don't think I've snoozed soundly for any extended time since I last bunked under my parents' roof in the days of longer hair and "The Moody Blues."

Whether it be for psychological or organic reasons, sleep and I, who used to be the best of childhood buddies, had become estranged. Although I do sleep better now than I did a decade ago, this winter has helped me ratchet it up another notch. For most of the past five or six weeks, I can manage only a few pages of reading before I have to snap off the light and roll over into a ball for a "long winter's nap." I haven't felt guilty one bit.

Rather than believe that this new-found joy for sawing lumber is due to age, that I am simply worn out by work and worry and now must resign myself to a recliner and television remote about the time the national news comes on, I suspect that just about as soon as the governor tells us we can spring our time forward and the grass is greening, I'll be back to my usual self, a yard rake in one hand, a golf club in the other. By then, I'll no longer bother with an alarm clock or go into mild shock when my bare feet hit the kitchen vinyl.

For the latest in sleep research, I turned to the aptly named Dr. W. Christopher Winter, who runs the well-respected Charlottesville (Virginia) Neurology and Sleep Medicine clinic. Winter, a board-certified and nationally recognized sleep medicine doctor and neurologist, appeared just last December on Fox News to discuss "microsleep" and shift-related work in regard to the tragic train crash in New York.

Winter tells me that my sleepiness probably has less to do with age (I keep trying to convince myself of that, too) than with the climate. In other words, if there was a winter that was tailor-made with a need to hibernate, this has been it.

"Sleep in the winter is probably better secondary to the reduced amount of sunlight," Winter told me. "That and the earlier loss of light and the colder temperature, facilitates sleep," he added.

In fact, Winter believes light, or rather the lack of it, plays the biggest role in making us sleepy earlier in the day. "In terms of light," he says, "it tends to block the secretion of melatonin, which is sleep promoting. The earlier loss of sunlight usually gets people prepped for sleep earlier."

Temperature also plays a significant part in our sleep. "With cooler temperatures, we find that humans tend to sleep better (bedrooms should be kept at 62-67 degrees) versus hot temperatures during the summer months," Winter says.

I obviously agree with the good doctor. It has been a sheer joy to be sandwiched between flannel sheets and cotton blankets, all warmed at body temperature, as I've listened in the dark to this year's winds and sleety snows smacking against window glass. We tend to keep our house frugally cool in the winter anyway — not a hard task this year at all — so perhaps the extraordinary cold of the now infamous "arctic vortex" has driven me to bunk and pillow more than usual.

At least three times a day this winter, I trudge my way to the barn to check on our aging recluse of a cat, Max. For weeks now, I have rarely caught him out of his bed, one that I bolstered with straw and a generous dose of heat from a dangling lamp, wired from a rafter above him. Max sometimes sleeps through my visits, getting out of the sack only when he is hungry for the canned food and warm water I deliver to him. He often looks up at me, squinting and grinning in the garish light of the lamp, pleased that he has such a comfortable spot in which to hole up until the real sun induces him to tan on our back deck. There is little doubt in my mind that he is sleeping at least 20 hours a day.

Dr. Winter tells me that melatonin levels affect animals, too, but often not for the good. Nocturnal animals, like raccoons, are stimulated to move around at night, which might explain why Max's food bowls are raided by some bandit while he gleefully dreams of slow-moving mice and pre-neutered heydays. The deer are also active; Joanie and I often see hungry bands of them, 20 or more, scrounging in the cornfields near our house, and not once have we passed by and not wondered at their ability to stand the blue crystal cold of sub-zero temperatures.

The sun is shining and the temperature has climbed to nearly 40 degrees as I sit at my window to write this. But the weatherman tells us that this thug of a winter is coming back to the neighborhood this week; within a few days we are to see a mean-spirited wind come calling in great shin-kicking gusts. Snow will apparently be joining the party, too, as will another spell of nose-numbing cold.

I still have to go to work, but like Max, I imagine that it would be better to just sleep in.

The Strange Case of the Lady in Shanghai

Instead of giving me a department store gift card or last-minute whatnot, my off-beat big brother, John, delivered a mystery to me last Christmas. It was the perfect present.

Tucked in the manila envelope he handed to me was a yellowed 8-by-10 black-and-white photograph of an austere, spectacled little man standing in a cemetery. At his feet lay a rectangular-shaped tombstone, and near it sat a wreath he had apparently delivered in formal top coat, tie, and spats.

"Okay," John said, "I know a little about what's going on, but you'll have to find the rest," as he grinned, knowing when I pushed aside a plate of yet-to-be-finished dessert that he had me hooked.

I imagine that we all have hobbies or interests that venture off the beaten path, and one of John's is no exception.

With the new-found time he's had in retirement, he often searches the Internet for old photographs that deal with Terre Haute history, and with this one, which is dated March 11, 1925, he knew he'd found a little cheap entertainment for both of us.

"I have no idea what cemetery this was taken in," he added, "but I have three names for you: Mrs. W.J. Snyder (the last name of which I could plainly see displayed on a larger family marker in the background), Baron Tanaka, and Saburo Kurusu. I can tell you that the man in the photo is Kurusu, a Japanese diplomat (an Associated Press note on the back of the photo told us that) and that he is there placing the flowers on the grave of Mrs. Snyder, because she somehow saved Tanaka's life in an assassination attempt. Have fun with it," he said, and went back to his pie.

I have had fun, and what I discovered, although tragic and solemn and involving the death of a talented woman whose family had already endured a painful string of tragedies, was a tale straight out of a Hollywood screenwriter's head.

One of the mysteries I first encountered about Mrs. Snyder was that I found at least three first names for her. Most newspaper accounts of her death identified her simply as Mrs. W.J. Snyder, the wife of a prominent coal mining executive from Brazil; she had been killed in Shanghai, China. But obituaries in the Terre Haute, Brazil and Greencastle papers alternately referred to her as Grace, Otela, and Otta.

But I get a bit ahead of myself, for how Snyder happened to be in the wrong place at the wrong time was the whole point of the photograph. Otela Grace Snyder, born Otta Grace Green near Chicago in 1880, was still very young when her father died, and she was sent to live with and be raised by an aunt.

After graduation from high school, she entered Hardin College, in Missouri, where she studied music, supplementing her schooling with lessons from noted performers from her hometown. After earning her degree, she accepted a position in the Lyceum movement and traveled throughout the country as a "reader" and musician; she eventually headed the Music Department at the Maryville Conservatory of Music.

In 1903, Otta Grace married Greencastle native Wilbur Starr, a "well-known evangelistic singer," and she began to accompany him on his travels, primarily in the Midwest. In 1916, Starr drowned when he attempted to ford a flooded creek near Chester Hill, Ohio, and his widow soon found herself living in Greencastle in the home of Mrs. Frank Donner, until she met Snyder, the vice-president and general manager of the American Coal Mining Company in Brazil. They married in Los Angeles on April 14, 1918, and within days caught a steamer to the Hawaiian Islands for their honeymoon.

Noted to be one of Brazil's "most popular and highly-esteemed" citizens, Mrs. Snyder's ability as a pianist and cellist took a "prominent place in musical circles in the city." It's interesting that Brazil had a very active arts community at the time, for Snyder was a member of the "music section" of something called the "LLS Club," and was in the "Women's Reading Club" and "Shakespeare Circle"; she directed the choir at the First Presbyterian Church, too.

An air of tragedy seemed to cling to the Snyders. W.J. Snyder's father had died on an operating table, and his mother succumbed after an accidental fall down a stairwell. Snyder's first wife died unexpectedly of heart disease in Florida in 1916, and in October 1920, his only son, Harry, and a nephew, John Zeller, were killed in an automobile accident as they returned home from Bloomington.

By the early spring of 1922, the Snyders appeared to have put their misfortunes behind them and were enjoying the last legs of a trip around the world; they had left for the tour from New York the previous October. In one of his last letters home before his wife's death, Snyder had described the wonders of Ceylon and announced the news that the couple was adding Shanghai at the last minute to their list of stops.

In what seemed to be no more than a stroke of misfortune in Shanghai on the morning of March 28, 1922, the Snyders were disembarking from the liner "Pine Tree State" at the same time as Baron Giichi Tanaka, a Japanese general, who at one time had been Japan's Minister of War.

Tanaka was a controversial man who had figured prominently in the Russo-Japanese War, had become a key political figure in Japan, and had actively promoted his belief that Japan needed to maintain a sphere of influence in Manchuria and the Korean peninsula.

Just as the Snyders and Tanaka reached the pier, two Korean nationalists — Jim Eak Sang and Au Soong Nyiun — threw a bomb at Tanaka. According to one account, the two would-be assassins, furious that the bomb had done no damage, then opened fire into the crowd around Tanaka, hitting Mrs. Snyder three times; she died a half-hour later in a Shanghai hospital. Tanaka was unharmed, and his two assailants were taken alive to stand trial in Kobe.

W.J. Snyder brought his wife's ashes home, and by early May a memorial service crowd packed their North Meridian Street house with mourners and flowers. On display there was a framed piece of white silk, presented to Snyder by the Korean Women's Patriotic Society before he left Shanghai.

"In memory of Otela Grace Snyder," its embroidery read, "who is mourned." On a note to Snyder, the women also wrote: "We most deeply regret the death of Otela Grace Snyder, who was accidentally killed at Shanghai by a Korean, who, because his people always looked to America and to the American people for inspiration and sympathy, and good will, would have no malice toward her, nor evil intent."

Tanaka went on to become Japan's 26th Prime Minister; he died at 63, not long after falling out of favor with Emperor Hirohito and the Japanese militarists who led Japan into World War II.

Kurusu came to Terre Haute three years after Snyder's death, upon receiving orders to make the stop on his way back to Tokyo from Washington, D.C.

He looked vaguely familiar in the photo to this history teacher, and turned out to be the envoy who not only signed a "Triparte Pact" with Nazi Germany and Fascist Italy in 1940, but also tried to negotiate peace between Japan and the United States, not knowing that the radicals in his country were planning the attack on Pearl Harbor.

I have seen a grayer version of him often in photographs with then-Secretary of State Cordell Hull. Kurusu spent the war in an American internment camp but was not prosecuted after the war; he died in 1954.

Like his wives, W.J. Snyder was nowhere near Brazil when he died. He passed near Ann Arbor, Mich., at age 83, and was brought back to Highland Lawn to be buried with the two women and a son who had gone on before him.

So, What Does Kindness Look Like?

There is an argument going on near my window sill. As I sit down to clack away at what will be a story about kindness, a squirrel and four blue jays bicker over a pile of birdseed I have left as charity.

I am not sure who will win out, but my money is on the jays, if anything, for their persistence and general orneriness. To have such acrimony in play as I write for what just happens to be "Random Acts of Kindness Day" is, I suppose, appropriate.

We read of wars and rumors of wars, of depravation and crime and meanness, every day in this newspaper, yet often we can also find stories on those very same pages about some deed of mercy or selflessness that, I hope, keeps a flame of kindness kindled in all of us.

In recent weeks, a local organization called SPPRAK (Special People Performing Random Acts of Kindness) has been promoting February as "Community Kindness Month," while Arts Illiana sponsored an art exhibit that asks, "What Does Kindness Look Like?" Despite the tag-team match playing out at my front yard maple tree that serves as a poor example, I want to try to answer that question.

I would like to think that I am a kind man, although in my line of work as a teacher, I am sure that I am often perceived as far from it.

My wife, my children, and every friend I have, to me, are kind people, giving and loving and considerate of others and the planet on which we trod. I've been lucky. I've had many people in my life who have been willing to lend a hand, even a shoulder, when I've needed it; friends who have called in tough times, lent when I was embarrassed to ask, given when they knew I couldn't pay it back. Above everything else, then, I think kindness looks like most of the people I've known, their smiles and laughs, their calloused hands and worn boots, their infinite good will toward stray animals and needy neighbors.

When I think of kindness, I remember the way my wife and I were raised. Neither of us had upbringings in wealth or privilege, but we certainly saw our parents and our grandparents as they gave of their time and money and labor to help others. My mom must have made an acre of pie crust in the name of charity and friendship, mended and made enough clothes to fill a department store, too. She did laundry for and lent an understanding ear to people she knew who needed it, and she believed that politeness and kindness were a way of living, not just an avenue to get what she wanted.

Kindness looks like my grandmother's diary, too. It is worn and old, undoubtedly purchased in a local dime store, and last written in by my aunt in the spring of 1971 when my grandmother could no longer hold a pen; she was just 60. In contrast to most of what I read in "social media" outlets — our electronic equivalent to diaries these days — there is no self-glorification in it. Each day for years, she recorded the day's weather, then wrote a few paragraphs about what she'd accomplished. I am amazed by it, and cherish it.

There is hardly a day that went by in my

grandmother's life when she wasn't doing something for her family or her church. It is almost dizzying to count the quilts she'd made, the meals she'd cooked, the gifts she'd bought, the floors she'd mopped, and the curtains she'd hung. Her days were filled with work, and much of it was in service to other people, people she prayed for and visited and worried over. Her face, a soft round Dutch face, is what kindness looks like to me.

Just a few months ago, it would have been hard to have missed the national news story about a 12-year-old Lakeland, Fla., girl who killed herself, allegedly after she had been bullied by more than a dozen other girls.

Rebecca Sedgewick, just a few days shy of her 13th birthday, climbed a tower at an abandoned concrete plant and jumped. Many of the text messages she had received from classmates at her former middle school were pinpointed as a probable reason. What had apparently once been a "boyfriend problem" had become fights and suspensions, and even an attempt by Rebecca to cut her wrists. The cyber-bullying continued, even after she left her school for another. Police also found evidence that she had been searching online for ways to kill herself. One thing that Rebecca's mother, Tricia Norman, told a television news reporter sent a chill down my spine. "Where does this hatred come from?" she asked. "Who is teaching these kids to hate?" When I read her words, I remember thinking, "Who had ever taught those children about kindness?"

When my mother was in the hospital on the last day of her life, I watched as a nurse came into her room. Dutifully, she checked the monotonously beeping monitor, saw to it that my mom had a full water pitcher, and almost as a reflex, gently pulled a wayward blanket across a foot that no one else had noticed was uncovered. It was a simple gesture, an act of kindness that couldn't possibly be repaid. It was, as Henry Clay said, one of those "Courtesies of a small and trivial character ... which strike deepest in the grateful and appreciating heart."

That is what kindness looks like.

The Long Goodbye to Winter

I have no idea what the weather is to bring to us on the morning this story runs, but on the day I write most of it, the sun is shining, and we have just come off a weekend of pleasant warmth and cloudless skies. Earlier in the week, a cold rain fell before yielding to an inch or two of snow, but it, and the foot or so under it, was finally washed away amid rain and wind and thunder.

The forecast now calls for a cold week, one where an icy finger of Canadian air waves itself under our noses again. These past few days are proof that when it comes to winter leaving us, it is almost always one step forward and two back. But that dance will change this month, and I am ready for it.

I have griped more about this winter's cold and snow

than most, but as happy as I am that February is gone and that March has now arrived kite windy, I wish to sing the praises of winter just a bit as we usher in this wet and temperamental new month. We have much to look forward to in the weeks ahead — the sounds of frogs and the sight of budding trees, being two — but I have to admit that I will miss the cold stars of clear cobalt-blue nights and the soft blankets of snow that time and time again this winter re-shaped the landscape in new and curious ways, and did so on silent feet.

One morning a few days back, I woke before the sun to put a pot of coffee to brewing and to fill my bird feeders. It was no surprise that I found it to be -5 degrees, but for some reason it came to me right then that it could very well be the last morning of the season that I was to shiver in such fearsome cold, and that the snow that I had shoveled from the paths to my barn and cabin the night before could be the last I would see accumulating for a while. When she emerged from a toasty bed a while later, I told Joanie that I planned to take a walk into the woods, despite the conditions, for spring would surely be here soon, and I wanted to catch the steam coming off the creek and test the ice that coated our modest little pond.

By the time I left the house later in the morning, my feet in dry, warm wool and my head covered with an ear-flapped cap that would make Holden Caulfield proud, I trudged through the back door of the barn and down into the woods behind it. I had a camera around my neck, a stout walking stick in one hand, and a pocket filled with extra batteries and spare gloves. The sun was strong and the sky was blue, and I could hear the crows cawing in tree tops a quarter-mile away.

Within minutes my face was red and my nose ran, and I was reminded of the mornings I got out of bed before dawn to go with my grandfather to run his muskrat traps on Spring Creek. Almost always I stayed overnight, waking to the intense heat of their coal furnace as it wafted through the registers, my grandfather banging doors and shoveling coal in the basement below me. I'd pull on cotton long-johns and buckled boots, and a coat two sizes too big, and off we'd go before my grandmother was up to make breakfast, before the sun was up to make light …

It was hard work at first to clomp and slide down our hillsides, but I soon found a rhythm in my walking and breathing, despite dealing with snow that reached my knees in some places and hid limbs and vines and holes that tripped me in others. As it often happens when I am alone with my thoughts, I began to think of things I've read, and despite it being some 50 degrees warmer than in Jack London's "To Build a Fire," a tale of the frigid and deadly Yukon, I pictured myself as the story's protagonist, "The Man." Despite being warned about walking the wilderness trails alone, his best-laid plans and early good fortune go for naught when he steps into a spring that silently runs beneath the snow. He fails to build a fire to warm himself, knowing as he drifts off into a frozen sleep that he should have heeded the advice of the "old-timers."

Since I planned to walk no more than a few miles north of my house, and was never more than half that distance to a well-traveled road, I didn't fear that my carcass would be left to the coyotes after my own misstep. My hillsides are dotted with similar springs that run year-round, mostly toward the Big Raccoon, but gurgle in places into sluggish brown pools. Knowing I could end up with wet feet and an uncomfortable walk home, I put my faith in the boots I had mail-ordered from L.L. Bean, spat into the air, and kept on walking.

My woods are a shallow lot; they empty onto an old railroad grade that lost its creosoted ties and iron rails like rotted teeth years ago. I walked that now rail-less trail north, realizing that I had started too late in the morning to see the vapor rising off the wetlands, for it was now a notch or two above zero. I came to the banks of our shallow mud hole of a pond, no more than three or four feet deep in most places, and gingerly stepped out onto it through a curtain of frozen horsetails, testing the ice as I went and recalling the winters I played with my sister and cousins in a similar place so many years ago. The deer had already taken liberties with the ice, and their trails dotted the frozen surface like meandering country roads.

Not far up the grade I found other tracks in such an oft-used and wandering trail that I couldn't figure out what had made them. They led me to a burrow under the reeds and into what may have been the remnants of an abandoned beaver lodge in the wetlands to the east. The marsh, normally alive with a chorus of geese and herons, ducks and mouthy blackbirds, was remarkably silent, the peeping of frogs and the buzzing of dragonfly wings weeks away, its water hidden beneath a coat of white frosting.

Playing the role of both explorer and snoop, I inspected cattails and grasses, the paper-thin and translucent leaves of beech trees, and the soaring branches of a massive sycamore, all before I came to a stream that pours out of the wetlands. I could see the water running freely under a coat of thin, clear ice, too thin to step onto. Out of curiosity I hammered the surface a time or two with my stick, setting off tremors of fracturing ice that ran both up and downstream in surprisingly loud pops and cracks, and the water bubbled through small fissures that I was certain would soon be re-frozen. It is an odd feeling to play a role in such a direct way, to disturb the natural order of things, but my mere presence in the quiet of the place had done that already.

In the distance, a woodpecker's pneumatic drill of a beak broke my reverie, so off I went again, this time toward the Big Raccoon at a pace fast enough to raise a sweat under my cap, and I wondered if a pair of cross-country skis would be a worthy investment next winter. Knowing from summertime experience that I could not cross the marshland to the creek without getting wet to the knees, I headed due north up the trail to catch the creek as it turns from the east, then makes a northwesterly run for the Wabash some two covered bridges and 10 miles later.

I was surprised to see that the creek ran clear, that not a single berg of ice floated along in its steady current. Shelves of ice along the banks and clinging to the roots of cottonwoods were thin reminders of higher water and even colder temperatures, and I stood on a bit of a bluff above the water and listened to the water slide by beneath me.

I knew I needed to head home, but like a boy who has been told to come in from the yard to wash up for supper, I dragged my feet in doing so. Knowing that Joanie would soon begin to wonder if I had been swallowed up by a sink hole or snow drift, I hiked across the road and climbed nearly straight up for a few hundred yards to find the old Coxville Cemetery blanketed in snow and silence. The graveyard is dotted with more stones than most would believe could be found in such a small place, but virtually all were hidden beneath a quilt of fresh white and only the hymns of the wind were played there. The tallest of the grave markers were visible above the snow and after an inspection of all I could read, I headed down the hill and onto the road for home.

Since I was alone and on the road on such a cold day, a few neighbors who drove by stopped to ask if I needed a lift. When I told them I was just taking some fresh air, I could see they were too polite to tell me that cabin fever had left me unhinged. I walked toward home across a ridgeline that is one of the highest in the county, stepping off into the woods more than once to look out across the fields below me, all the while watching a solitary hawk hang suspended in the cold air as if attached to invisible wires.

There was much to see at walking speed that I miss in the blur of a moving car. I could see the tracks of the deer we watch at twilight as they root through the tundra of the fields searching for the corn the combines missed in the fall, and I could see that even before the roads thawed they'd be a mess of potholes and crumbling pavement. I idled past a farmer friend's equipment sheds and grain bins, his empty hopper wagons waiting for the harvest of crops yet unplanted. It was a balmy 11 degrees when I walked up my own drive, a chorus of blue jays reminding me that they'd already emptied the feeders and were expecting a second course.

The poet David Budbill reminds us that winter is "the best time" to discover who we are. In the "Quiet, contemplation time/away from the rushing world ..." we can find our "inner landscape." I don't know if that was true in my case for these few hours; I thought of nothing in particular except how beautiful it was to be out and about on a cold, clear day.

It was all a part of my long goodbye to the winter.

Something to Crow About

It is in the spring, I think, that I notice crows the most. They are noisy neighbors year-round, but they come calling (I resisted saying "cawing") in early March in earnest, and they do so before the frogs on our pond and the buds on our trees make the new season official.

I noticed quite a congregation of crows a few days ago as I clomped from bedroom to kitchen in house slippers. I passed the trio of tall windows in our living room and saw more than a dozen just wandering around in the back yard as if they'd lost a wallet or dropped a set of car keys. They were remarkable birds, all about the same size, with the demeanors of morticians on burial day, appearing very solemn and grim, although I know from personal experience that they are no such thing.

I saw even more just an hour or two later as I backed out of my drive to head to my son's place. There, just down the road, a good quarter-acre of my neighbor-farmer's barn lot was a sea of undulating black as a whole school reunion of crows bumped and ground themselves together as they gleaned spilled corn from the ground around the grain bins there. I can't imagine a single kernel being left behind and would have hated to have been the cop trying to manage the riot.

Farther down the road I saw yet another cliquish bunch

milling about in the stubble of a soybean field, most not bothering to flap themselves even a few feet farther away at the sound of my truck. Since the deer have given that field a pretty good going over all winter, I can't imagine what they were finding of interest there.

The American Crow — *Corvus brachyrhynchos* to ornithologists and bird watchers — is found from British Columbia to Florida. Crows are a hardy bunch that have adapted themselves to the human condition quite well; every continent, save South America, has at least one variety of crow to call its own. They are omnivorous, eating anything from leftover fast food to road kill to aquatic plants, and they are smart birds — among the smartest — that gather in roosts that may have over a quarter-million members, and can, if caught early enough, make entertaining pets.

There are more crows now than at any time in history, primarily because there are more of us. As mightily as we may want to rid ourselves of them from time to time, for they have done more for power washer sales than just about anything else alive (perhaps starlings trump them all), crows have come to live near us because humanity's very nature is to leave things around for them to eat, and to build places in which they like to stay.

We create the roadside carrion on which they feed, leave our garbage out as free buffets, and have, over centuries, killed so many of the raptors and other predators that curtailed exploding crow populations that we are quite responsible for helping their progress.

Crows, like the ones I saw that day in my yard, are big birds. They can be nearly 20 inches long, and they are prolific when it comes to reproducing. It is interesting to note that some unmated crows serve as "helpers," devoting some of their time to raising other birds in the roost — adoptive or foster parents of sorts.

Large, extended families of crows spend their nights together, then head out in smaller groups to search for food. They've been known to cover 50 miles or more on these foraging parties.

I have spent some time with crows myself. I remember when I found a crow in the middle of the road on the way back from a trip to the creek for a swim; I was about 12 years old. He'd apparently been knocked silly by a passing car, and I asked my dad if I could take him home.

After a few weeks in a cage that we'd built first for our pet raccoon, and with me nearly force-feeding him bugs and berries, he finally took off for places unknown, but not before I'd come to admire his stately deportment and cold, black eyes. Crows, ravens, and jackdaws are related; as "corvids" they share considerable talents, as well as looks.

Crows like to collect and hide shiny objects, particularly aluminum foil and soda can pop tops, even jewelry. I know the latter is true, for a friend of my dad, a local tavern keeper, kept a crow that once brought a quite decent wristwatch into the bar to show off. I could just see its owner searching below the window sill where'd he'd left it, perhaps even pointing an accusatory finger at a neighbor.

One of the very best sources I could find about crows is *In the Company of Crows and Ravens*, by John Marzluff and Tony Angell. Marzluff, a professor of Wildlife Science at the University of Washington, loves crows — finds them fascinating and entertaining creatures — and has spent considerable time observing and studying them.

Just last week, Marzluff told me that crows "...are important ecosystem engineers: recycling waste to enrich the soil and providing nests for other species (for example, small owls make themselves at home in old crow nests). Second, they are emissaries from nature that because of their brash actions remind us we are just one of many species... ."

He went on to add that crows are "...very much like us [humans], and therefore, as sentient beings, they simply deserve our respect and compassion. ... In my lab, we've learned that they use their complex brains to store and recall a lifetime's worth of knowledge gained from personal experience, and from the observation of other crows."

Marzluff, of course, isn't the only admirer of crows. There is little doubt that they can be pests, and we test them to seek the spread of West Nile disease, but they have undoubtedly become part of our culture, as well.

We often "eat crow," have "something to crow about," use "scarecrows" in our gardens, use "crowbars," look long distances from "crow's nests," develop "crow's feet" as we age, and measure distances "as the crow flies."

Marzluff's book tells me that the earliest artists painted crows on cave walls, while other peoples carved them into totems; Noah counted crows to find land in the midst of the Great Flood, while other peoples yearned for their wisdom. Shakespeare mentioned crows in his plays, and Schubert depicted them in his music; Alexander the Great ignored the crows at the gates of Babylon and was warned of his doom for doing it; Van Gogh painted them.

Surely, it is well known that a flock of crows is called a "murder," but why is very much debated. One explanation comes from an old belief that crows would congregate to decide the fate of an unruly or thieving member; another belief originates with the fact that crows can be found among the dead of battlefields.

It is a warm evening as I put this piece to bed; my window is open, and I hear the last honks of the geese on the pond below our hill. But tonight, I sing the praises of the clever crow, who despite our best efforts at scaring him off, is here to stay.

In his ***The Art of Seeing Things***, the old naturalist John Burroughs wrote, "I venture to say that no one has ever heard the crow utter a complaining or disconsolate note. He is always cheery, he is always self-possessed, he is quite a success."

A Book Inscribed is a Book Treasured

I don't think it's a secret that I value books as one of life's great joys; "I am, therefore I read," could be a T-shirt-worthy motto of mine. Besides reading them, my wife and I also collect them; some to give away, others to keep as long as we breathe.

Buying books has become nearly an addiction for us; just ask our floor joists as they moan every time we return home from a trip to our favorite bookstore, or our children, who ultimately will have more than a few of our keepers on their hands.

Among the most endearing things about used books for us are the inscriptions we find inside their covers. We buy a good many "pre-owned" books at stores and auctions and garage sales — have quite a few given to us, too — and we've often found them to have been inscribed by givers to readers under all circumstances and of all ages.

Whether they've been gifts at Christmas or birthdays, for children or sweethearts or dear old friends, a good inscription can make a book special, can help bring it to life, can provide intrigue and interest and motivation to even the most reticent reader.

Some of them make us feel a little sad, too, for we know that the book was given in sincerity or love, yet tossed aside thoughtlessly by someone who forgot that a grandparent or parent gave them the book years before. Of course, in many cases, there simply was no one left to take ownership of the books, and they've been tossed into boxes to mildew in damp basements.

As much as I've tried to like e-books, I still feel that a real book is a thing made of paper and ink and glue; they are physical, as well as intellectual things — we can feel them, touch them, hear them... I've published a few books, myself, and plan to get after writing another this summer — a book from scratch, as opposed to a collection of stories. So, I spend considerable time, pen in hand, inscribing copies for people who buy them, and for those to whom one is given. It's my hope that the readers stop to read the inscription I've left for them, for I truly do mean "Best Wishes" when I sign one with those words. Of course, they may have to decipher my scribbles before they know it.

I have trouble thinking of good original inscriptions for my books. One of my biggest concerns is that I might misspell a name or omit a crucial word, particularly in the rush when I have interested buyers waiting in a line for their turn at the table. I refuse to hand to a reader a book in which I've committed some egregious error — an inscription ruined by a sudden loss of ink or an inadvertent smear made as I've dragged a hand across a page. "A few stories from my home to yours," reads one of my favorite inscriptions. I mean that, too, for it is an honor to hand a book to a reader and know it is going home to live with them.

Although there are thousands and thousands of books on countless shelves for me to read for the first time, I have to admit that pulling a book off my own, then opening it to see an inscription, makes me want to re-read it all over again. That happened to me just yesterday. Despite having a stack of books in my house that I have yet to tap into — my wife claims my now-infamous piles are actually booby-traps that collapse when only she walks by them — I pulled a copy of David McCullough's "Truman" off a cabin shelf and opened it to see my brother's familiar and perfect handwriting: "To Brother Mike ... Happy Birthday! Sept. '92," it read. I recalled, just for an instant, how much I enjoyed that book, all 992 pages of it, and even where I spent a few of my days reading it. It made me want to sit in lamplight and start it again, but I appreciated even more that it was my big brother who gave me the book.

One of the first books ever given to me as a gift, besides those from my mother, came from Ruth Hallett, the wonderful lady who helped me start my life as a teacher many years ago. Before I left her mothering care — she suspected I had never stayed away from home for long, but had to while I did my practice teaching — she gave me a copy of the works of Nathaniel Hawthorne, for she knew I loved his short stories. "Best wishes for a future in teaching," she wrote. "I have enjoyed getting to know you." I've been told that dear Mrs. Hallett still volunteers her time at the school, and that wouldn't surprise me at all. Her inscription still makes me think of her and that school and those days.

I have become somewhat enamored with a website, the "Book Inscriptions Project" (www.bookinscriptions.com), a site dedicated to the art of writing messages in books, which shouldn't be confused with merely signing a book or autograph collecting. There are hundreds of images of book inscriptions on the site, started twelve years ago after its founder, Shaun Raviv, discovered a particularly intriguing message inscribed in a used book. I've spent a lot of time on that site just scrolling through inscriptions, realizing that it isn't always the author of a book who is sharing the wisdom or knowledge or plot.

I have to be careful; once I start writing about the feel of a book in my hands or the countless hours I've spent curled up like an old cat enjoying one in the quiet of my house, I can go on and on. There's more to life than good books, but I have to say that, for me anyway, a good life has always included them. Knowing that many of my books were given to me by people who knew I'd be enjoying them, and telling me so inside their front covers, well, that just makes the reading that much better.

'At the End of the Day, Smell Like Dirt'

I woke up with the morning sun in my face a couple of Saturdays ago, a rare thing considering I have grown accustomed to being at work before it is up, and the habit of being awake early and in darkness has carried over into my weekends.

But that week was different; it was the first day of a badly needed break from my day job, and although I didn't believe I could, I managed to sleep through the ringing of the imaginary alarm clock I have set in my head for years.

With every intention of accomplishing something, I went to sleep the night before with thoughts about being outdoors, digging in the dirt and trimming brush and raking flower beds and getting my chainsaw fired up.

It was the second day of official spring, so I wanted to be up early, eat breakfast with purpose, and be outside while I could still see a little of my breath in the air. I'd hear the crows having their usual early-morning conversations and surprise the cats with breakfast a little earlier than they are used to on the weekend.

Instead, I lolled about and stretched a while and peeked through the blinds at a blue sky, and eventually wiled away much of the morning with my newspaper and coffee cup as companions. Not unlike an old bear, I took my time in waking up to spring. It even took a while to make out a list of things I wanted to do with the day, for I didn't want to make it too long.

But once I got outside, I made up my mind to get things accomplished, and quickly set about working as if it were to be the only nice day of my vacation, as if "killing snakes," my grandmother used to say.

What I couldn't have known was that my unconscious forecast proved to be mostly true in the long run, but on that day, the sun shone, the temperatures climbed into the mid-60s, and with each half-hour or so, I found myself shedding layers and gloves and heavy socks like some rube fan dancer. For the first time in months, I worked up a sweat at working.

I decided that before I'd ever get my lawnmower out from under its winter tarp to service, I'd rake portions of my yard, amazed that, despite having it picked clean when I put my tools in the barn for good last December, it was now littered with the usual leftovers of the coldest season — buckets of acorns and half-eaten walnuts, twigs and pin oak leaves, the scrub and scruff of the wind-blown and brittle dead.

I cleaned gutters and swept the deck, re-stacked rock and raked the iris beds, even walked along the road to collect and haul two wheelbarrow loads of pea gravel and dirt clods left in the grass by an unrepentant snowplow.

After a lunch reminiscent of my days as a kid — one involving just a few gulps and a little fidgety table conversation — I was back at it, trimming back brush from a fence row (I cut saplings and vines away from two nice patches of raspberry briars), used a pole saw to take out a few low-hanging limbs that consistently knocked off my hat last summer, then tackled a scruffy hedgeapple tree behind my barn that had been begging to become firewood for years; its wish came true.

The arrogance of a warm early spring day led me to take my snow shovel to the barn, to sweep out the garage, to open the windows to my cabin, and to mow the long ornamental grasses in our garden with the saw blade I keep on my weed trimmer; I lopped off the crowns of last fall's mums, as well.

By late afternoon, I was tired; my back ached a little, and as is customary, I realized that I'd nicked myself with the tooth of a resting chainsaw and suffered a small but painful cut in a middle finger, a mystery injury that stung and bled until I finally asked Joanie for a bandage.

It seems to be a genetic disposition in our family that, if work is to be done, the men of my lineage must bleed while doing it. My son proudly carries on the tradition; by mid-April or so, his knuckles will be scabbed and his arms scraped by brushes with tillers and mowers and saws. We either throw caution to the wind or are extremely clumsy, whichever it may be.

My first real day in the spring sun is a day for seeing what I either look past or is hidden under winter snowfall. When all is melted, I see just how close the deer come to our house on winter nights. The proximity of their hoof prints in the mud had me wondering if they have been window-peeping.

That day was also right to see a half-dozen of last year's bird nests, to pick up twigs by the armloads, to check if the trees I planted in the late fall were greening. While I was at it, I decided to get our bird boxes up and open for new residents. Each spring, it seems as though I consider their housing a little later than I should, but on that day, I remembered to double-check my fall cleaning and repair, then get them back — sitting atop galvanized pipe or fence posts — into place so our bluebirds and wrens and titmice come to spend the summer.

Last year, it seemed as though we had an unusual number of phoebes and grosbeaks about, too, and since they like to nest under the eaves of my barn and in the lower trees along my woods, I am hopeful that nothing I have done in my spring cleaning disturbs them.

I sat a brand new cedar nesting box out with every intention of staining it and nailing it to my cabin that day, but when evening came, I saw that I had forgotten the project altogether and had to leave it for another day.

As an orange sun began to dip behind a smattering of western clouds, I recalled that just a few Saturdays before, we had been anticipating six inches of snow, and got most of it by morning.

Just as I was slipping off my boots in the garage, Joanie came through the door and asked when I wanted to go for a walk, which we did, although my tank was precariously close to empty before we ever put one foot in front of the other.

The writer Margaret Atwood wrote, "In the spring, at the end of the day, you should smell like dirt." I'm not sure what I smelled like after my first spring day out and about my place, but I was more than dirty enough by evening to have smelled of the soil that was ground into the knees of my jeans, the soles of my boots and the creases of my hands.

But something an old friend, Donna Harrison, relayed to me later that evening rang even more true.

"I needed some sunshine on my shoulders to make me happy," she said.

I'm in the Philippines; Send Your Money

Well, first of all, I am not in the Philippines, nor do I ever want to go there. It would be too ironic, particularly if I am robbed and beaten and need help from my friends.

If you have no idea what I'm talking about, then you've probably never sent an email to me, because if you have, you'll have recently received an urgent plea from my wife and me as we tell you a sad tale of misery and misfortune, then beg for money.

Please don't respond; it's a scam. In an attempt to pry cash out of the wallets and purses of my good friends, someone hacked my email account and sent a note to all my contacts, suggesting that if you ever want to see me in the States again, you'll help keep me out of a Filipino jail. Why, those dirty scoundrels at the hotel we're staying in are holding our luggage until I pay my bill, and my flight is leaving in minutes. I promise, I'll pay you back if I ever get home. So far, they may have collected about $1.78 because none of my friends and relatives have real money anyway.

I think that I was most surprised that many of my fellow emailers have never gotten one of these letters before, and I'm thankful that my particular version wasn't one touting the newest male enhancement drug or youth-defying face cream; it simply hopes you'll give these crooks access to your credit card number.

It is, however, refreshing that in one afternoon, I heard from cousins I don't get to see but at reunions, old friends from out of state who wanted to "let me know," even business associates who thought that "perhaps I should do something about it."

In a single day, I received phone calls from my doctor, several readers, co-workers, and folks with whom I go to church. I am thankful that so many people were watching my back; I really am.

So what have I done in response, except wish I could get my bony fingers around this hacker's throat? Well, according to Adam Levin, the founder and chairman of Credit.com, the first thing anyone who gets hacked should do is change his or her password information.

If I actually lose my email account because of this —
that is, the hacker takes control of the account — I need to
contact my email site help center and have them get it back
for me. The least anyone should do if they've been hacked
is contact their email provider and make sure they know.

I had several friends wonder if my getting hacked was
perhaps related to recent security breaches with big
companies like Target and Anthem. I have no idea, but
those companies' assurances that they are doing everything
they can to protect our identities and personal information
rings a bit hollow to me; kind of like thanking someone for
watching the barn after my horse has already been saddled
and trotted off.

Levin also suggests that a hacked emailer needs to let
all his contacts know he's been hacked; I hope I am doing
that now. He also thinks it's a good idea to scan your
computer for new viruses and spyware, review your
personal email settings, change passwords for other sites —
without repeating them — clean your own email folder,
and, finally, monitor your credit and financial accounts.

Other than those things, there's little else I need to do,
except perhaps toss my computer in the trash and begin
writing with a quill.

So, finally, I just wanted to let you all know that we
are fine, and if we take a vacation anytime real soon, we
promise to go no farther than Peoria. But if I am ever

mugged anywhere in a foreign land, I swear that I'll drag myself to the American Embassy and spare my friends the desperate pleas for wire transfers and credit card numbers.

Now, if you still want to send a check to me, I won't complain.

The Most Important People in the World

I don't know if any of you read the story on the Huffington Post a few weeks ago about Quincy Kroner, a two-year-old Cincinnati boy whose interest in trucks — the local garbage truck, in particular — led him to an experience he isn't likely to soon forget. I also wonder that if you did read the story, whether you reacted to it the same way I did.

In mid-March, Quincy got to meet his heroes — two neighborhood garbage men named Mark Davis and Eddie Washington — who happened to be thoughtful enough to take the time to wave to the little guy each week as they dumped the Kroner's trash cans.

Quincy knew when to expect the truck to come each Friday and apparently found a spot near a front window to watch Davis and Washington do their jobs and wave as they got back into their truck.

Quincy's dad, Ollie, says his son has been "fascinated by the garbage truck" since he was old enough to walk, so he took Quincy out to meet Davis and Washington, who stopped working so they could have their picture taken with

Quincy as he held the toy garbage truck he'd received for successfully tackling potty training. By the way, he was so overwhelmed by the experience that he cried as the photo was snapped.

I loved Quincy's story, mainly because — and I suspect the same is true for you — I had more than a few Marks and Eddies in my life, too: adult men, and women — often complete strangers — who bothered to be kind, to wave, to speak to a curious little kid who thought that something as mundane and smelly and loud as a garbage truck was about the most captivating thing in the world.

It wasn't a trash truck I was interested in as a boy; besides waiting to chat with Walt Williams, our mailman, just about every day, I loved to watch the road workers as they came by our house on the County Line Road.

I am just old enough to remember when that road was paved for the first time, and with each subsequent re-surfacing, ditch-cleaning, or pot-hole filling, I had a front-row seat on our hillside to watch the comings and goings of graders and pavers, trucks and rollers. I think I can still smell the mildly noxious odors of road tar and truck exhaust and gasoline, and hear the rattle of pea gravel roaring out of the heavy iron dump truck gates, and the rumble of revved engines as they bore down on steamy asphalt.

Without reminiscing so much as to get young eyes rolling, I have to add that our lives in the country then weren't exactly filled to the brim with excitement, and if a hard-hatted road crew and their yellow dump trucks and the crush of graded gravel was what my day had to offer, I took it in as if going to the circus.

My mother often told the story of her frantic search for me one summer day when I was five or six. After exhausting every nook and closet in the house and basement, she finally found me under a huge burr oak amid a crew of road workers as they sat in the grass to eat their lunches.

I was going from one to the other grabbing up Twinkies and crackers and apples that the men willfully handed to me, and I think I can still see myself, resplendent in green canvas bibbed overalls, holding my stash like pirate treasure.

Mom was embarrassed by my brazen act of beggary, but more so that the men may have thought I wasn't being fed enough, so she served them all iced tea and a slice of pie before they headed back to work. It was not the last time they stopped for a break in our yard, and Mom allowed me to take them ice water in an old aluminum cooler I rolled out to them in a red wagon.

I remember, too, a wonderful week when my dad hired a carpenter named Bruno Iacoli to replace the door and windows of our old front porch. I couldn't have been a whole lot older than I was when I captured my booty from the road crew, but I sat and watched and talked to Bruno so much that he eventually asked me to hand him tools or pick up bits of wood, probably just to keep me out of his way.

He was a good guy, and he took the time to show me a bit about using a carpenter's measure and a level. I thought him to be one of the most important men in the world, admiring the pencils and knives and gadgets he endlessly pulled from his overalls pockets, the sawdust heavy on his thick, brown arms, and how he cuffed his pants and drank coffee from a Thermos.

When my kids were little, I often asked them what they wanted to be when they grew up. My daughter, a speech pathologist now, said she wanted to be an electrician, for she always did her best to get strings of old Christmas lights to work. She wanted to hunt rocks for a living, too.

We still remember the day Ellen stood looking over Joanie's shoulder as Evan fed on a bottle. Joanie asked Ellen what she thought Evan would be someday, and after a moment of thought, she said, "I don't know, but I hope he doesn't want to be a burglar."

We didn't worry about that too much, but we were mildly surprised when Evan maintained by the time he was six or so that he wanted to pursue grocery bagging as a career.

He's a financial adviser now, but I'd still bet he would have gone to the limit to protect eggs had he become a pro bag boy. My wife said he also was interested in pursuing a job as a floor sweeper at basketball games; I imagine that it did look like fun.

I don't think it's important that we know what we want to become in life — I'm not even sure we ever really get it figured out. I doubt that Quincy will become a garbage man or even drive a truck for a living, although it would be just fine if he did.

The most important thing is that we keep fostering our kids' imaginations for things like trucks and electricity and grocery bagging, even for road paving and level reading, by being like Mark and Eddie and Bruno and that crew of tar-spattered laborers who rested in our yard.

But please, don't beg for food out of people's lunch boxes.

One Man's Trash Is Another Man's Trash

Many people are growing weary of ecological doomsdayers, and if so, they are the folks most likely to tell us that Planet Earth isn't in that bad of shape, that it can repair itself, that new technologies just around the corner will solve our carbon emissions and greenhouse gases and oil consumption and the ever-growing pile of plastic in which we are drowning.

But after just one afternoon of picking up roadside trash along my property a few weeks ago, you'd have a hard time convincing me of that ...

On what turned out to be the only decent weather day of our spring break a few weeks back, Joanie and I, tired of looking at the litter that had accumulated along the decrepit old woven-wire fence that runs north along our property line, decided to make part of our daily walk a cleanup detail.

Armed with three plastic garbage bags that were big enough to hold junked Pontiacs, and clad in gloves and sweatshirts, and sadly, when considering the date, long johns, we headed off to police the roughly two- to three-tenths of a mile that our woods run along the blacktop. Needless to say, we underestimated just how much time we were to invest, and how much trash we'd discover.

Since we are experienced trash pickers from way back — I take great pride in picking up even gum wrappers and cigarette butts from my yard — we didn't start out that late morning already disgusted with the task at hand at all. We have gotten into the habit over the years of recycling about everything we have in the way of trash, some of it, such as aluminum cans and newspapers, going to the Terre Haute Humane Society; cash from the cans they recycle buys dog food, and the newspapers are used as cage liners. I have often wondered if passers-by see us walking along the roads in the early evenings, a half-dozen crushed beer cans in our hands, wondering if we've both developed serious drinking problems, but that hasn't deterred us from doing what we think we should. We are, after all, notorious neatniks.

Both of us possessed a sort of optimism as we walked

to the end of our yard and headed up the road that day, but it didn't take long for us to realize two things: First, we either were going to need more bags, or my wheelbarrow, or perhaps a neighbor's grain truck. And second, we both were going to be too tired and too short of time to actually take our regularly scheduled walk that day; there was that much trash.

I think our haul was impressive, and insulting, and, in the long run, a bit depressing. On just our side of the road, and in no more than about 1,500 feet (we did venture about six to ten feet into the woods to retrieve well-thrown and blown refuse), we picked up 241 plastic, clear, brown, and green glass bottles, 217 aluminum soda and beer cans, and at least one overstuffed 55-gallon plastic bag of fast-food wrappers, Styrofoam, prescription pill bottles, cigarette packages, car parts, smokeless tobacco cans, a calculator, two T-shirts, a shoe, two sheets of tin roofing, and three concrete blocks. Our little crusade took us more than three hours, and as the minutes ticked by, I grew more ticked off. How could the people who drive by just these few feet of woods, I wondered, many of them people I know, be so lazy that they couldn't have at least taken their own trash home?

Our friend, fellow walker Carol Groves, asks that question every time she wanders from her house in town out into the country, often with another friend, Shirley Chaney; they bag trash as they march along. Carol told me one day last week, "I just can't stand to look at it." It is not uncommon now that she knows the shelter can use the cans, for us to come home to find a bag of aluminum that she's left for us by our garage door. Her effort, by the way, provides a candlelight of hope in the face of all the trash we see.

It is staggering what we Americans throw away, most often without thinking about it. Americans represent about five percent of the planet's population, yet we generate about 30 percent of its trash. Of all that garbage, only about two percent of it is recycled. For all inhabitants of the world to live like Americans, we would need two more Earths; in a lifetime, we each will throw away about 600 times our own body weight.

Take those soda and beer cans, for instance. Americans toss enough of those into trash cans — or out their car windows — to rebuild the entire commercial air fleet every three months. One ton of recycled aluminum saves us well more than 1,600 gallons of oil; there is no limit how many times it can be recycled. As for all that glass we picked up, well, Americans throw enough of it away every week to fill a 1,350 foot-tall building. Plastic is even more disposable for us; we toss enough of it each year to circle the Earth four times. Only 25 percent of all the plastic we could recycle is recycled. If we recycled the other 75 percent, it's estimated that we could save a billion gallons of oil.

No one is asking us to read **Silent Spring** this week or

to spike trees or harass Japanese whalers or join the Al Gore Fan Club. Picking up our own trash, and trying to create a little less of it, would be a nice start to cleaning up the planet, maybe our own back yards, maybe even my fence row. It isn't a radical idea or environmentalist extremism, and it shouldn't pit us against one another, either; it's common sense.

My calendar reminds me that Earth Day is coming on April 22, the 44th such celebration since it was founded by Wisconsin senator Gaylord Nelson. He tried to remind us four decades ago that we have only one Earth and that we need to take better care of it. He said: "The ultimate test of man's conscience may be his willingness to sacrifice something today for future generations whose words of thanks will not be heard."

As a way of promoting that first Earth Day celebration, cartoonist Walt Kelly, already well-known for his work, drew his philosophical Everyman possum, Pogo, as he looked out across his home, a trash-strewn Okefenokee Swamp. With head in hand, he mutters, "We have met the enemy and He is us."

Pogo was right, and his simple words sure beat what I was muttering along the road the other day.

"Thoughts that Breathe"

Against the backdrop of dogwood white and redbud lavender, I watched a chickadee come to inspect a recently cleaned bird box that sits atop a pole near the edge of my woods. In the green background and through open windows, I heard a phoebe as he let me know that he was home for the spring from points north, where he winters. It was, to say the least, a day nearly poetic.

The scene reminded me much — if for no other reason than the latter bird is mentioned — of a poem I often hear in my head: Robert Frost's "The Need of Being Versed in Country Things." I love the poem, for it represents a blend of two topics I most enjoy: the green of the country and the sounds of pondered words that have been knitted together like a favorite scarf.

Like the land under our feet, we do not appreciate poetry as much as we should. I agree that it isn't as newsworthy as the latest headlines, but it is one thing — in my world anyway —that makes such news more bearable, and sting less, discourage me less.

April should make us happy for a number of reasons. Tucked under its blanket of overturned soil and irises and budding leaves are last week's Earth Day and World Reading Day and a National Library celebration. April is, as well, National Poetry Month, and surely old weather-worn and exhausted English teachers, as I most certainly feel by this time of year, are celebrating, whether they are allowed to teach much poetry anymore, that is.

I am a simple-minded man, so I don't clutter my life with the hassles of reading poetry I don't much understand, for I will take a challenge only so far. That is my mindset when I dust off my Robert Frost and Emily Dickinson, my Ted Kooser and Linda Pastan, to give my students a sample, nearly begging them to give that gang of wordsmiths a chance. After all, they aren't really that tough to comprehend, and the pay-off for sticking toes into their versed pools can be mighty.

Poetry will never put money in my kids' pockets. Of that fact they are reminded often, perhaps before they sit down to take a standardized exam, which might contain, if they are lucky, an excerpted stanza or two of poetry set amid a field of mostly bland passages. I understand that such reading, if clearly recalled, supposedly makes them much more employable.

Perhaps, if I have time this year, I will share with them the story of Lucy Larcom. Born in 1824, she began working in the brutal textile mills of Lowell, Massachusetts, when she was just 11 years old. Her father, a sea captain, died when she was eight, and her mother, unable to make ends meet with a boarding house business, saw Lucy and her older sisters and brothers — she was the ninth of ten children — quit school to go to work.

Larcom was a "doffer girl," filling the deafening machinery's empty bobbins for hours on end. She worked in the factories for ten years, yet managed to produce dozens of poems and songs and letters that described her life of labor. Her poetry attracted the attention of the legendary poet John Greenleaf Whittier, and she was eventually able to quit the factory, move west to become a teacher and writer, and become an advocate for the girls who worked as she had.

Larcom wrote: "I regard a love for poetry as one of the most needful and helpful elements in the life-outfit of a human being. It was the greatest of blessings to me, in the long days of toil to which I was shut in much earlier than most young girls are, that the poetry I held in my memory breathed its enchanted atmosphere through me and around me, and touched even dull drudgery with its sunshine."

She also wrote: "The soul, cramped among the petty vexations of Earth, needs to keep its windows constantly open to the invigorating air of large and free ideas. ..." That we do, and that is why I still teach poetry, and I feel quite fortunate that where I teach, I get to do it. Poetry shows our children the language, its power and grace, its rhythm and music; it is essential.

I have often quoted that old Swede, Carl Sandburg — whose home we visited as we drove through the Illinois prairie last summer — who said that he'd "written some poetry I don't understand myself." And so, I tell my kids that it's all right if they don't understand all the poetry that they read or write themselves. Poetry is a way for us all to learn the beauty of figurative language, a way to swallow big ideas in small doses; it is a way, for some of my students anyway, to make sense of the world, whether it be through their own words or those of someone else.

In the past year, I have tried to write a little poetry myself. Perhaps it is just an old man thing, an attempt to rope more words into a different corral. I am no Frost, no Walt Whitman — although I am beginning to look more like them with each passing year — and in echoing what is often repeated, I will probably never make a dime in doing it.

Thomas Gray, a poet who I do not often understand, said, "Poetry is thoughts that breathe, and words that burn." So, now that I think of it, I believe poetry is far too important to waste on all those standardized tests.

Miss Kinsey's Forsythia

It always seems like it's Sunday when we notice Miss Kinsey's forsythia. Joanie and I will be driving home from church, most often with our car windows down so we can enjoy springtime breezes and smells. And then, as we are talking about nothing in particular, we catch it in a passing flash of yellow and green. We have never known it not to be there.

Elizabeth Kinsey lived in Coxville in a small, white-clapboard frame house, first with her parents, then with her aging mother only, and then on her own. She seemed like a Havisham-like character to a young girl like my wife, in the days when she'd tag along with her handyman dad to look after the old lady's clunky television or wind-blown antenna.

Miss Kinsey liked flowers, but didn't necessarily like to get dirty, so, it is likely that within just a few feet of her windows, it was her parents—Charlie and Agnes—that had planted forsythia, which Joanie says couldn't have been nearly as tall as it is now.

All that is left of her house these days are a few chunks of foundation concrete, for falling into disrepair in the years after Elizabeth closed her beauty parlor and moved into Rosedale a few miles south, the place eventually took on an air of abandonment. I can't quite recall, but it seems to me it finally disappeared as bonfire kindling 20 years or so ago, leaving behind a few daffodils, a bit of ivy, and a little Sweet William.

For the most part, Miss Kinsey's small lawn is now just an overgrown patch of brush and weeds and roadside trash.

I am fascinated with such simple stories. There once was a house and a kind old lady who lived in it. And now, we see only the overgrown spot where both home and owner once stood, it in hardware-store paint, her, perhaps, in a cotton house dress. But despite its scraggy appearance, her forsythia has stood the test of time, a monument to the family that lived and gardened on that spot. It makes me wonder about the years ahead, perhaps long after my house is gone, as to what will live on that my hands have touched, planted, nurtured, built.

This year has been a tough one for forsythia. I have several stands of it myself, and it seems as though the few sprigs of gold they had were replaced by tiny lime-green leaves in a matter of just a day or two. Usually, its flowers are around long enough for us to enjoy a week or more, shining like back-porch bug lights amid a sea of greening springtime grass.

It is much more usual for us to be complaining this time of year about our magnolia, which bursts like popcorn in a display of fragrant white blooms. But its flowers never stay for long: a chilly April night or windy cold front nearly always decapitates its prettiness too soon.

This year, however, it has been in bloom for nearly two weeks, its flowers just now giving way to new leaves in the warm sun of an Easter Sunday afternoon.

I have been taking stock this week as to which plants of mine made it through this killer winter, and which didn't. I have a few tulips that have endured near our mailbox for more than 30 years now, and despite rude blasts of road salt and gritty sand, and an untended home in our hard yellow clay, I see they are up and ready to bloom in the next few days — ten to twelve red buds growing bolder and bolder.

But the hens-and-chickens in both our big pots, despite being under the barn roof and protected all winter, are as dry and dead as fall leaves; Joanie will have to start those from scratch.

The English ivy that crawls up our storage shed and covers the hillside near my cabin has had a very slow start, too, so slow, in fact, that I find myself breaking a vine or two every so often just to see if there's any green to be found in it.

Several big clumps of ornamental grass, and a butterfly bush that I nursed back from the dead just last spring, are goners, and we've lost too many chrysanthemums to even count.

Along the back roads we drive, we find spots where houses once stood. Lilies and daffodils and peonies dot the landscape in places where driveways once found their way to homes and where tillers strained against the earth.

Fence posts, too stubborn to drop over, still stand, gate hinges hanging from them like rusted tongues. The ghosts of houses still hover in those places, perhaps the laughter of children, too. I hope that will not be the fate of my place; I have worked hard here and want someone to take over where I leave off, someone who will fight the good fight.

In Ray Bradbury's great *Fahrenheit 451*, a book that the author, himself, believed would help him "live forever," a character named Granger speaks of his grandfather. His words are among my very favorites.

I have used them before, but they are worth repeating again: "Everyone must leave something behind when he dies, my grandfather said. A child or a book or a painting or a house or a wall built or a pair of shoes made. Or a garden planted. Something your hand touched some way so your soul has somewhere to go when you die, and when people look at that tree or that flower you planted, you're there. It doesn't matter what you do, he said, so long as you change something from the way it was before you touched it into something that's like you after you take your hands away. The difference between the man who just cuts lawns and a real gardener is in the touching, he said. The lawn-cutter might just as well not have been there at all; the gardener will be there a lifetime."

I have a feeling that Miss Kinsey's forsythia will be there a few more lifetimes, too.

Walks in the Woods Go On

By a stroke of the calendar's timely hand, I always have a story that runs on the Monday morning following Mother's Day. It may very well be a too-late topic in the "What's new?" world of journalism, but since I write to the beat of a slower drummer than most columnists, I can't pass up the opportunity to say a word.

For the third time in three days, I am headed to the woods this morning, not with any real goal in mind, although I do have a bag shoved into my back pocket just in case I happen to find a mushroom or two.

It is just that after a winter of some discontent — one of feeling penned like a 4-H rabbit — and a job that keeps me at a desk late to grade essays and plan lessons and write the occasional story, I simply need the freedom our hillsides and redbuds and redwing blackbirds can afford me.

My mom taught me to love the woods; not my dad, who loved to hunt, or even my grandfather, who was obsessed with being outdoors with a fishing pole or hoe or bag of ginseng root in his hands.

Each spring, at the time the woods were waking up to warm air and the calls of new birds, my mom would pack a few paper bags with sandwiches and take me to the rolling patch of wildflowers and red oak behind our house.

Every year since her death, I write about my mother; it is the least that I can do. Well, perhaps the most I can do, actually, other than to keep myself out of jail and pay my taxes on time.

I still remember those spring walks we took, the peppered egg sandwiches, the thermos of warm water, the apples that she packed. We'd sit under the same big tree every year to eat and gab, and we got to know each other in those days. I was lucky, for knowing her wasn't the same as just living with her.

Because of her influence, I still have a favored walking stick to use as I prod and poke under leaves and lift ferns and whack offending briars or low-hanging limbs that need pruned back from our paths.

And, I am still amazed at the same things she was: box turtles and black snakes and new leaves and mayapples and snails. For all of those interests, for a life of books and walks and trees, I will be eternally grateful.

I may not have known it then, but our walks in the woods were the best classrooms I ever entered. There is value in the serenity of a forest, the simplicity of rocks and bark, the smell of soil and wood rot and branch water that teaches us more than any lecture or worksheet or video can. There, the closeness to the basic parts of living things gives us an appreciation for the bigness of the universe, because only by looking at the parts can we get a sense of the whole. Getting down on one's belly and looking at the life teeming in a handful of dirt or the wonder of the veins in a single leaf can be exciting things.

Our woods this year have been beautiful, and I have taken to packing a camera with me instead of a lunch, for taking pictures has become somewhat of a new passion for me, while I have always had a natural talent for eating. It feels good to stretch my chair-bent legs, to breathe in air scented by dogwood and the countless wildflowers — the anemones and wild geraniums and violets and sweet William — that have been resurrected by the warming soil.

As more Mother's Days pass without her, I know that somehow, someway, my mom knows how life has been for us, how things have turned out. She probably knows that she is about to become a great-grandmother again, that we are happy, and that we have had good lives.

This time of year, I'm happy to think that she knows

just how much I still love walking in the woods, and I am thankful that she first led the way.

A Face Only a Mother Could Love

It is fitting that Mother's Day comes when it does, for spring is a maternal season, one for new beginnings, for birth and rebirth, for flowering and nurturing and caring.

Each year, it seems, I have a story to write for the Monday after Mother's Day, and each year, I write about my own mother, who, perhaps more than anyone else, I wish I could speak to again. I'd hope we all think of our mothers that way. But this story will be about mothers other than my own.

Of her, I will simply say that she was a pie-baker, a clothes-mender, a scolder and hugger, a Bible-reader, and good friend. She was as tough as nails but as delicate as a lace doily, a wonderful person who was often too critical of her own faults. She was my first and best teacher, and she's never allowed death itself to stop her from dispensing lessons to this day.

I have been taking stock of other mothers in my life right now, two of which have come to live in my barn a while.

Of course, I'm not speaking of my wife. If a major argument were to ever separate our sleeping arrangements, I think I would be the one making a bed in the straw we keep there, not Joanie. Luckily, that has never come to pass.

I am speaking of two temporary inhabitants at my place: one an unnamed and uninvited little cat who, by the looks of her, is going to give birth any day; the other a young mother possum who already has seven mouths to feed, and is managing to do that with the help of our table scraps and leftover cat food.

This has been a year for stray cats at our place. Old age and attrition had reduced our population to just two felines as the fall crept into winter.

Our indoor cat, Edgar, spends his days at our window sills sunning his black fur and capturing imaginary prey; he's a manic bundle of nerves, but we've made him our own.

The other, of course, is the ever-present Max, who has survived a litany of scrapes with mean strays and car bumpers and quiet garage doors for 15 years now. His only concession to old age has become the heat lamp he expects over his bed when the temperature dips into the low teens, and despite a rather low IQ, even by tomcat standards, he manages to hang on year after year.

By January, however, we had picked up a rather brutish and sore-footed vagrant we began to call Leo, since he resembled a lion. He has never moved past the curmudgeonly stage and, on occasion, plays the role of schoolyard bully to our other cats.

Next, we picked up a bleary-eyed orphan that I named

Earl, somewhat, I suppose, after the dim-witted former felon of television reruns. He has already made two trips under protest to the veterinarian, and I often look out the window just in time to see Joanie traipsing after him, eye-dropper in hand, hoping to get a bit of medicine into him.

Then, of course, came Miss No Name, who Joanie agrees will have to stick around long enough now to deliver and then wean her litter. She'll then face a quick spaying before we shuffle her off to a new home; after all, we can't keep them all.

I was, however, more than a little surprised a few nights ago when, as I headed toward a shower with the dust of an evening yard mowing in my hair, Joanie told me she intends to keep one of the cat's kittens. I can recite chapter-and-verse my reasons why we don't need another cat to care for, but I don't believe I have much say in the matter.

The possum has been a most unusual guest. Living where we do, we often get the occasional raccoon or skunk or snake or possum hanging around our barn like hotel lobby guests. She has taken quite a liking to that aforementioned bed of Max's.

Just the other day, I slipped onto a mower and fired it up for an hour or so of grass cutting, and as I pulled back, I saw a long pink snout pop over the top of the bed, a bungee cord-like tail soon following it. I turned off the mower and peered into the bed to see her, yawning and sleepy-eyed, seven white and black babies, so ugly they are cute, curled up around her for a warm afternoon nap, apparently not concerned I was watching. I found it odd to see the inner toes of her hind feet work in chimpanzee-like nimbleness, and soon had my wife and visiting daughter in the barn to see the show.

I have written about possums before, and I know of the hazards of allowing her to stay around. Her razor sharp teeth keep me aware that she'll never be a pet, nor would I want her to be. But, other than losing a bit of cat food to her, she seems to be doing us no harm, and when she and her babies move on — and they will — I'll get Max a new bed.

Besides, her offspring may have faces that only a mother could love, but love them she must for they will be her traveling companions for three months or more, hitching rides on her back or on her tail until they are big enough to take care of themselves.

I am not particularly happy that I am operating an animals' home for single mothers in my barn, that a no-name cat, thoughtlessly dropped out of someone's car like garbage, has brought her problems to my doorstep. And, that a possum, one of the most homely and nearly prehistoric of creatures on the planet, has made herself at home, too.

But the good mother I live with now will not turn them away, and the mother I had as a boy wouldn't have either. So they can stay on a while.

There is an essay, called "Our Mothers," by the long-gone Christopher Morley that I read last week for no particular reason. In it, he wrote that mothers "created our world, and taught us to dwell within."

I think he was right about that.

A Mushroom Story You Can Actually Believe

Everyone knows that avid mushroom hunters are, at least when it comes to how many they've found and where they've found them, inveterate liars. Less than forthcoming with directions and pertinent landmarks, the typical seekers of springtime fungi have no intention of truthfully answering inquiries as to where and when they've filled their bread sacks. I am no different.

So all I will say about the where of an interesting find my wife, Joanie, and I made a few weeks ago will probably have to go to our graves with us. But the what, well, that's a different story.

We are an odd couple when it comes to mushrooms. We both love to hunt them, but only Joanie craves them on the supper table. I have never liked the taste — or rather, the lack of it — of mushrooms. Flour and salt and pepper and butter all you want, but I'm not, and never have been, a fan of fungus; I have faced derision for this apparent flaw for years. But hunting mushrooms is a passion, so we spend a little extra time in the woods in April and May, searching for that magical patch of morels that most "roomers" only see in their dreams.

By most accounts, this wasn't a great year for morels; perhaps the cool spring contributed to their paucity; I haven't heard nearly as many people bragging about their hauls this time. I suspect that hunters merely recycle photos from their bountiful years, just to keep their rivals wondering about the site of that secret mother lode.

But we are going to crow a bit this year, not for the big sponges we found, but for the two mushrooms we discovered in searching for the elusive morel. After spending the best part of an hour with no success at all one day a few weeks ago, we descended a slope in our woods with every intention of making our way to a nearby wetlands to see if we could spot a turtle or heron or colorful dragonfly. Ahead of Joanie by some distance, looking, I believe, up into an ancient sycamore tree at a nest, I heard her say, "I think you need to come over here and look at this."

A deer skull perhaps? A bit of trash? Maybe a snake? Those were the thoughts that first crossed my mind when I heard her, that is until I saw the subject of her intense focus: a weird orange mushroom growing out of a rotting, barkless branch near the much larger corpse of a fallen tree. I'm not exactly a character out of a James Fenimore Cooper novel, but I've spent my fair share of time in the woods over the years, and I had to admit to Joanie that the mushroom she'd found was unlike anything I had ever seen. Since I have gotten into the habit of carrying a camera on my hip, I snapped a half-dozen shots of the fungus, and after a few more minutes of wondering just what we had, we moved on.

By the time we got back to the house an hour or two later, I looked at the photos of the mushroom, convinced by then that I needed to get it identified, so I sent two of the pictures off to Dr. Peter Coppinger, an associate professor of biomedical engineering at Rose-Hulman, who just happens to have his PhD in plant biology. Within 20 minutes, Peter responded that he really hadn't seen anything quite like it himself. He asked a colleague, who also hadn't seen our mushroom before.

Coppinger's interest was as piqued as ours, so he eventually got in touch with mycologists at the University of Tennessee, and only one had laid eyes on such a mushroom. Coppinger related, "It is extremely rare; so rare, that most field biologists haven't seen this except in pictures." He said that the mycologist who identified it relayed his congratulations to us for a "very special find."

What we stumbled upon is called *Rhodotus palmatus*, an uncommon species of mushroom that was originally given the name *Agaricus palmatus* in 1785 by French botanist Jean Bulliard. Its name was changed in a 1926 publication by French mycologist Rene Maire, and it carries a number of nicknames, such as the "netted rhodotus," the "rosy veincap," and the "wrinkled peach."

As it turns out, there's a very good description of our mushroom in a Wikipedia entry, and a number of other fungi-related websites that I visited listed it too. The rhodotus is "saprobic," that is, it gets its nutrients from "decomposing matter," which explains why we found ours growing out of a rotting tree branch. It has apparently been found growing on basswood and maple and horse chestnut trees, but is more commonly found on elms in heavily shaded and wet woodlands; some mycologists even suggest it is a byproduct of Dutch elm disease.

The most interesting thing I discovered about rhodotus is that it's found most often in places like Poland, even New Zealand, but it is classified as "rare" in the United States. It is found in North America, and Indiana and Illinois seem to be the most popular spots. Conflicting evidence exists about its edibility, but since I have a standing policy against taste-testing what looks like a glorified toadstool — and I have seen things growing on shower room floors that look about as appetizing — I decided to take a pass.

I have to give Coppinger a lot of credit for taking his job seriously. Within a few days, I was leading him and his professional photographer father, Jim, to the spot where we had uncovered the rhodotus — in fact, two, since we discovered another one growing under the limb the next day. Jim, who dressed the part and looked like he was straight out of "Mutual of Omaha's Wild Kingdom," spent over an hour taking dozens of photos of the mushrooms, lying on the chigger-infested ground snapping shots from every conceivable angle. I also introduced the pair to some of our steeper hillsides, which made both consider hiring a Sherpa if they make a return visit.

In a way, it was too bad that we got our mushroom identified. In the back of my mind, I saw the Lunsford name emblazoned in the print of musty mycological guidebooks forever. Move over Carolus Linnaeus and Alexander von Humboldt, the Lunsfords are here!

Just don't ask me to eat what we find.

"Spring and Her Hem of Wildflowers"

Spring, it seems to me, took its good time in getting here; we got at least one extra inning of what has been called "dogwood winter," and I wore long-sleeved shirts until mid-April. But, when it did come to us, it came overnight. One day I saw barren trees and brown grass from my windows, and the next morning I awoke to a sea of green. As is customary, I have begun to spend more time in my woods, and in doing so have found interesting things in ordinary places.

On one of those walks a few weeks ago, before the woods had come completely alive with most of the things that bite or itch, Joanie and I pulled on our blue jeans and boots and went for a walk, descending our hillsides, some so steep we had to do it sideways; like wary old hounds, at times. It proved to be the best therapy for what ailed us both: Too busy schedules and not-enough-time-in-our-days, which are two man-made afflictions that we hope to remedy as soon as the school year ends, although I doubt we'll ever be completely cured.

With a camera in hand I followed her as we walked down the path first cut through our property in the old railroad days more than a century ago, for the ridge we live on at one time was dotted with coal mines and bisected by a spur of the long-gone Vandalia line that ran through Rosedale to Roseville to Mecca and points north. The trail was used, I am told, to drag equipment to and from the road to the west, and one story I heard suggests that even a house still used nearby was pulled up that narrow trail with a team of oxen and replanted where it still stands.

On this day, we first avoided the open spaces of the old railroad bed and opted to walk to a meadow of sorts just to the north of our house, one that was dappled with sunlight as it filtered through a grove of osage-orange and hawthorn trees. Along the way, we saw slabs of soft sandstone jutting out of the hillside like bucked teeth, and nearby a young black snake lay coiled like a dark hose still sleeping off his winter grog. Joanie realized that she could have stepped on the snake and began to pay considerably more attention to where she planted her feet.

We eventually hooked up with the interstate system of deer trails that took us down even more slopes to wetter ground, through a stand of wild rose bushes to a place where mayapples grow along the hillsides like miniature tropical forests, and the ground is littered with the dead branches of long-downed elm and sycamore trees, now depositories for lichens and mosses that redefine what green really is.

From there we headed south into one of my favorite places in the woods, for it is spotted with young beech trees and the ground is carpeted with wildflowers — the white of anemones, the deep purples and greens of prairie trillium, and the blues of marsh violets. The sun played with the clouds and the light moved across the whole scene as the trees creaked in the breeze. Joanie and I had run through our conversations a while before that and were content with our own thoughts and the songs of mockingbirds and thrushes; we heard the woodpeckers drilling away at the dead trees that stand in the wetlands to our east. Despite not knowing what we were hearing, a Northern Parula was calling out to us too. We have heard them before, but have never seen one, for they stay high in the tree canopy; my daughter, who is quite the birdwatcher, identified it for us later.

From there, we walked the well-trod railroad grade, lined on each side by horsetails, and there amid a watershed created by hillside run-off and springs that bubble out of old mines long collapsed, we saw places where the iron-tinted water left rusty-red silt clinging to last year's submerged leaves, creating a palette of color that will remain, for the most part, unnoticed throughout the year.

In all, we spent three hours in the woods, and our legs grew weary as we climbed the ridge for panoramic viewpoints, then descended to the mush of wetter ground to catch the scents of old leaves and mud. We heard the screech of frogs as they let us know we'd come too close, watched dragonflies — armored as if ready for a joust — as they bobbed and wove with one another over cattails. We spied a blue heron overhead as he tried to fold his legs underneath him like passenger jet landing gear, picked up stones, inspected deer and raccoon tracks, and stayed well past what my watch was suggesting we should.

In her poem, "Spring," Linda Pastan writes, "Just as we lose hope/she ambles in,/a late guest/dragging her hem of wildflowers…" I'd say she got that about right.

Work Ethic Travels Over the Years With Bus Driver

I've spent a lot of time with Tom Scamihorn over the years, most of it sitting in the right front seat of a school bus while he drove a load of loud kids down the road to a ball game, museum, or academic contest. You get to know

173

a little about a man when he's behind the wheel next to you, particularly one who's lived an extraordinarily active life.

Tom is retiring this year — not earth-shaking news, in itself, when I consider that three of my other friends are also moving on in their lives, and one is even a few weeks younger than I am. But Tom is different; he's had so many jobs in his lifetime that he can't remember them all. He's driven a bus though — often on a route, but mostly for field trips and to sporting events — for the last 22 years, not a remarkable thing unless you consider that he didn't really begin driving for Southwest Parke Community School Corp. until he was 66 years old.

At 88, Tom has no intention of giving up his driver's license anytime soon, nor should he. In fact, he's planning to just keep on working around his place, cutting wood for his stove and mowing a little grass and driving wherever he needs to go. He lost his wife, Genevieve, last August — they'd been married 64 years — and thought for a time he'd sell his big place and move closer to his daughter, who lives in Columbus, Indiana. After all, they had been making that 240-mile round trip for visits together every other weekend for more than 20 years anyway. But for now, he's going to stay put. "I have plenty to do around here," he said.

Tom amazes me; he goes where he wants to go, does what he wants to do, and eats whatever he wants to eat. I don't think he knows what it is to take a pill or go to the doctor. An avid wood-cutter and splitter — he's heated his rural Parke County home through his own labor — he can hardly recall a day in his life when he didn't feel like working. He "retired" from Alcan (now Novelis) once, then went back for another five years. "I went back because I liked the work and liked the place," he says. He spent 10 years there as a maintenance man, but then served as a supervisor for 15 more.

"Oh, I guess I have never really retired," Tom added. "I've been busy my whole life, and I want to keep being busy."

Although there's no way of knowing how many miles Tom has driven his school buses, it is true that a conservative number of the field trips he's chauffeured is well over a thousand, his last coming May 15 when he took the track team for a meet at Seeger High School, a long drive that involved a late night.

"I enjoy driving," Tom said. "I enjoy being around the kids because they keep me young. Bob ("Goose") Yowell asked me to drive for him years ago, and I told him I'd give it a try. I didn't know it would get into my blood and that I'd be doing it this long."

Tom has been a lot of places in his life besides those he's traveled to by bus. After his mother died when he was 15, he left Terre Haute with a sister to live with an uncle in Indianapolis. "My dad worked hard, but there were six of us, and he didn't make enough to feed one," he said. "I guess I've been working since I was about six," saying he remembered selling eggs out of a bucket through the neighborhood to make extra money for the family.

Tom's time in the state capital didn't last long. He walked out of his classes at Broad Ripple High School in 1943 to join the Navy at age 17. "It sure was different for a 17-year-old kid like me to be on a big ship out of Pearl Harbor," Tom said. He was aboard the USS Boggs, a destroyer that had served part of the war as a minesweeper, but was a destroyer again by the time Tom was on her. "We weren't in any big battles, but we chased a few subs around; we did our part," he said

Back in Terre Haute after the war (he was discharged in 1946), Tom went right to work. He held down jobs at the paper mill (several times), the heavy water plant near Newport, worked construction in West Virginia for a year, then finally got on at Alcan. He told me that he and Genevieve had some "hard times" when they were young, and he knew that work was the only way out of them. "Besides, I like to work," he said.

In a few more years, there are going to be even fewer men like Tom around. It is a staggering fact that nearly a thousand veterans of the Second World War are dying every day in this country. But I don't mean only that this "Greatest Generation" includes those who served in that greatest of wars. It was a generation of men and women who believed in working, believed that to earn their own keep and make their own way was the only way to do things. It is the trait in Tom that, perhaps, I admire the most.

When I think of Tom, it makes me even more appreciative on this Memorial Day for the men I've known who are a lot like him. Men like Dick Howk and Bill Engle and Perry Huxford and Leighton Willhite, who, near or past 90, believed in fighting for their country years and years ago, but then came back home to lives of hard work. What examples they've been to me, and to a lot of others.

When I asked Tom to tell me what it meant to serve his country during the war, what it meant to him to be a veteran, he hesitated a while and simply said, "Well, it's kind of hard to put into words."

It sure is.

Noticing the Lowly Dandelion

I'd be a liar if I said that I miss the yellow carpet of dandelions that dotted my front yard just a few weeks ago. As is the case every spring, I patiently mowed and snipped and clipped them — even dug more than a few out of my flower beds — then waited for their blooms to change to puffy white seed heads, which signal the end of their glory for another year.

I have never sprayed my lawn with herbicides to kill dandelions because I've always tried to avoid using much of anything that has a skull and crossbones on its label, and because I rarely see honeybees anymore, a bad omen, I fear, of things yet to come for us.

No, I won't say I'm upset that the dandelions have, for the most part, taken their leave; I like a nice uniform, green lawn as much as anyone. However, that doesn't mean I haven't come to respect this tiny flower, and those disappearing bees, both of which possess a lot more power than most of us probably know.

Like most children, I once thought dandelions were about as pretty a flower as there could be, but also like most, I was raised to consider it a weed, something of a nuisance that was to be pulled or sprayed, a temporary plaything that came each spring, but was gone by the time the summer heat had really set in.

I knew even then, when dandelions "...had changed from suns to moons," as the writer, Nabokov, once said, that my interests would move to other things, like the smell of sassafras, or the cool mud of the creek, or the taste of ripening pears on my grandmother's big, old backyard tree.

My interest in dandelions has, however, been rekindled after I spoke with Anita Sanchez, an author, educator, and blogger from New York, who has spent a lifetime exploring the "unmowed corners of the world."

If you want to know anything at all about dandelions, then reading her ***The Teeth of the Lion: The Story of the Beloved and Despised Dandelion*** (McDonald and

Woodward Publishing, 2006) is the place to begin.

"The thing that struck me about dandelions is how human attitudes towards them have changed over millennia," Sanchez told me. "They're one of the most ancient plants used by humans. Ancient Greeks and Romans, and others for many centuries before them, used dandelions — leaf, root, and flower — to treat a host of ailments. They seem always to have been a sort of green first aid kit. The roots stimulate liver function and help filter toxins from the body — a crucial function these days when we're besieged by toxins in our water, air, and food."

I have known for years that dandelions were used by herbalists, like Doc Wheat, the eccentric local Parke County, Cincinnati-trained eclectic, who put cowslip and black cohosh and lobelia and a host of other local plants, like dandelions, to work in his elixirs and tonics. I knew that folks resorted to eating dandelions — violets and other yard "weeds," too — during the Great Depression when food supplies dwindled to nothing. But never in my wildest dreams did I know that dandelions are actually about as nutritious as any plant we have available to us, and that at one time they were cultivated.

"Dandelions were one of the first European plants imported to America, probably on the Mayflower. They were planted as crops, sold wholesale as medicine, judged at county fairs and planted in gardens for their cheerful yellow beauty," Sanchez says. "Gardeners used to weed out the grass to make room for the dandelions. It wasn't until the 20th century, when Americans began to seek a pure, uninterrupted stretch of green lawn, that dandelions became 'Public Enemy No. 1,'" she added.

She's not exaggerating. About 30 million acres of this country are devoted to our lawns (I feel I sometimes mow about half of them myself), and 80 million pounds of chemicals, costing about $40 billion, are dumped onto those yards each year, mostly in an attempt to control the lowly dandelion. Obviously, the investment is a temporary fix.

Sanchez writes in her book: "We rarely notice dandelions these days, except when we try to kill them. ... But still they follow us, down the centuries; they stick to us as closely as a dog, as inevitable as a shadow. We may try to outrun them, but we never will; they are our footprints.

"The thing that actually got me to sit down and write a book on dandelions was the appalling statistic, that, according to the Audubon Society, more than seven million wild birds die annually because of the aesthetic use of pesticides. Aesthetic use — not growing crops to feed hungry people — poisons we use to make our lawns and gardens look nice. Every spring you see those little yellow markers warning people to stay off the lawn for 24 hours. ... But who can't read those markers? Birds, butterflies, cats and dogs, barefoot toddlers — the potential effect of pesticides on the developing nervous systems and organs of children is frightening," Sanchez says.

Being a bacon-and-eggs man probably doesn't make me want to run out for a dandelion salad anytime soon, or take dandelion-enhanced supplements, but apparently they'd both do me some good. Sanchez tells me that weeding gardeners probably pull the most nutritious plant out of their soil when they remove their dandelions.

A "vitamin powerhouse," a hundred grams of raw dandelion greens have 14,000 international units of Vitamin A and 35 milligrams of Vitamin C. That's seven times more of the former (pound for pound) than oranges, and more of the latter than tomatoes.

Years ago, I read Ray Bradbury's ***Dandelion Wine***, a magical semi-autobiographical novel that captures the love the author had for his hometown of Waukegan, Illinois — the love he had for his own childhood, really.

Setting his story in the summer of 1928, Bradbury wrote, "Lilacs on a bush are better than orchids. And dandelions and devil grass are better! Why? Because they bend you over and turn you away from all the people in the town for a little while and sweat you and get you down where you remember you got a nose again."

He also tells us: "Bees do have a smell, you know, and if they don't, they should, for their feet are dusted with spices from a million flowers."

The Mystery of C.C. Kelso

This is no thriller, no locked room puzzle. It isn't worthy of Arthur Conan Doyle, won't win an "Edgar" for mystery writing, either. But a small brass plate bearing the engraved name of C.C. Kelso adorns a picture that hangs on our family room wall. How it got there, and the identity of Kelso, provided us with an enigma of sorts, one I finally managed to solve just last month.

As improbable as it sounds to us now, it has been nearly 40 years since Joanie and I, in the first few days of our long teaching lives, first saw a beautiful sepia-toned print of Sir Galahad that hung in the old Montezuma High School. Perched near an ancient and wheezing water fountain, the oak-framed picture got our attention every time we stopped to get a drink, which was fairly often in those pre-air-conditioned times. After seven years at the school, consolidation moved our careers a few miles south, but neither of us forgot Galahad, who had apparently looked over crowded hallways of children by then for nearly 60 years.

The print was dedicated to Kelso by the Class of 1922, and although the name on the plate — attached to the frame with two small screws — meant little to us, we told principals and janitors, teachers and even superintendents that if the picture were to ever be taken down, we'd like to buy it. But Galahad remained in place for years more, that is until an extensive remodeling of the school led to its disappearance. We thought we'd never see it again, for no one we asked knew what had happened to it.

We never forgot Galahad, though, or Kelso, who we speculated had probably been a student at the school, suddenly swept away perhaps by accident or influenza or war. Over the years, I made half-hearted attempts to discover who Kelso was, and what had happened to the print. I uncovered no leads, though, until 2009, when I decided to call Paul and Diana Bartlow, both loyal members of the school's alumni association, and two people who, it seems, always have their fingers on the pulse of whatever project or program that is good for the small Parke County community.

Diana told me that she did, indeed, know what happened to the print: "It's in our garage," she said, "in pieces... Paul found it in a Dumpster." By then, he had come to the phone to tell me — my jaw still near the floor — that the print had been damaged by rainwater and sun, that the frame was broken, and that the glass was gone. "I just couldn't let it go to the dump," he said. I promptly offered him a decent donation to the Alumni Association, and in an instant became the owner of that which we'd always coveted, albeit, water-stained and dirty and in shambles.

With a little elbow grease and steel wool, a bit of wood stain and Brasso, I soon restored the beautiful "tiger oak" (made through a process called quarter-sawing) frame (which is over four feet tall) and Kelso's nameplate. But knowing I needed an expert to put the critical finishing touches on the project, I added another hero to my short list alongside the Bartlows.

Tina Blackburn not only owns Professional Glass in Clinton, but also she's the best I know at framing and mounting artwork. Upon seeing the old print, she told me that she thought she could "touch up" Galahad's water stains with charcoal, and that she did. When I walked into her Ninth Street shop to pick up Galahad a few weeks after I'd dropped it off, it looked better behind its new glass than it had in all those years next to the school water fountain. But I still had work to do. Who was C.C. Kelso?

Our particular Galahad image has a long history. Originally, it was a painting done by the great English artist and sculptor, George Frederic Watts, in 1862. "Sir Galahad" was a large, colorful, dramatic piece done during the artist's Romantic period, but Watts was eventually swept up in the Symbolist Movement a few years later, famously saying, "I paint ideas, not things."

By the 1890s, Galahad was being widely reproduced, most notably by the Prang Educational Co. in Boston, which is exactly where our print originated. It, and a series of other pictures depicting heroes and legends, was incorporated into school curriculums in those days — something sadly lacking now.

Although I had dabbled in researching Kelso, I really went to work just a month ago. While Joanie was running errands, I spent some time at the Rockville Public Library, and the good folks there led me to not only an index of county obituaries, in which Kelso turned up, but also microfiched copies of the defunct "Montezuma Enterprise," which was, surprisingly, in production until 1951. It took no time at all to find Kelso's story.

Cecil C. Kelso was not a student at Montezuma High School, as we had theorized; when he died, he was in his fourth year as the superintendent of all Reserve Township Schools. He was just 34 years old when he lost his fight with diabetes on the morning of Feb. 6, 1922.

Kelso was born in tiny Rush Center, Kansas, in 1887, grew up in only slightly larger Ireland, Indiana (in Dubois County), and attended Indiana University before graduating from Indiana State Normal College in 1918. He had apparently taught nine years in Ireland before he ever completed his university degrees. After the funeral, Kelso's body was taken overland to Terre Haute, then loaded onto a train, which took him home to Ireland. He is buried there in a churchyard cemetery.

As was noted in his obituary, C.C. Kelso "... was a man of strong mind, high ideals, and great courage." He was praised as a "vital force for good," and it was noted that the minister who presided over the funeral said, "You will be missed, for your seat will be vacant. A prince of

Israel has fallen today. ..."

Well loved by the students and faculty at Montezuma, Kelso was honored within weeks by the school's senior class of just seven students. One of those seven was Claude Billings, who eventually became a longtime reporter and book reviewer for our Tribune-Star. Ironically, Joanie and I visited his book-crammed home in Montezuma not long before he passed in 1985.

If only we had known to ask, he could have told us all we wanted to know about C.C. Kelso ...

Invitation to Skinks Stops at My Door

Living as we do, near the woods, we accept the fact that the occasional mouse or snake is going to make its way into our house. Although I have worked pretty diligently over the years since we bought our old place to plug every crack and cranny I can find, I imagine that somewhere in our crawlspace there remains a tiny door mat near a knothole or sagging joist that reads, "Rooms Available."

But when my good buddies, Joe and Dennis — and the host of other friends who helped build my small writing cabin — were hard at work a few summers ago, I told them that one of my top priorities was that I wanted no unwelcome guests making their way inside, so we were going to fill every cleave, cleft, and crevice we could hunt down. I wanted no repeat of the early years in our house when we could have billed it as a herpetarium.

Despite the few lady bugs and ants that have made their way through my cabin door, I haven't had that first field mouse or garter snake, despite being situated just a few feet from acres of woodland. But I did have a visitor last week, one I'd seen outside not a week before, and I am now under the sneaking suspicion that he has back rent to pay.

I have been hard at work on a book. It isn't the one I keep promising everyone that I am making progress on, but rather my fifth collection of stories. In these first few days I have been away from school this summer, I have been diligently clacking away on my keyboard, burning the midnight oil while formatting and editing and re-writing. For the most part, the only sounds I hear besides my own rumbling belly and the whir of a ceiling fan, are those of the birds and the breeze on the other side of my window screens.

It was only after I began rummaging around one day in an old Hood River Apples crate that I refinished a few years ago to serve as an antique filing box that I caught a flash of blue and black out of the corner of my eye. And there, just under a pile of manila folders and spare copy paper, I found my tenant: A relatively large blue-tailed skink, more appropriately called the American five-lined skink. I think he (or she) had been making himself at home, for he seemed to already know my floor plan. As soon as I

187

reached for him, he headed straight for the door as if a hotel guest who had memorized all fire exits; all I had to do was open it.

Skinks are speedy and elusive, and despite being among the most common lizards on the continent, they tend to live nearly invisible lives. Their habit of basking in the sun, as if working on their tans, makes my place a most hospitable home for them because one of their favorite habits includes stretching out on warm rocks during the heat of the day.

Because I am an old rock hound, and have lined nearly every flowerbed and garden border, and even filled the spaces under my decks, with split sandstone, skinks must like it here. And because those spots attract crickets and spiders — at the top of the typical skink menu — I imagine they like it all the more.

There is remarkably little mention of the five-lined skink (*Plestiodon fasciatus*) on the Indiana Department of Resources site, but skinks seem to have made quite a splash in places like New England and Canada, primarily because they are becoming less and less common. Typical that we humans tend to cherish things only after we realize that they are nearly gone.

Lower skink populations may be just one more harbinger of bad things to come for our planet, because they tend to be environmentally sensitive. Ironically, it appears that they do tend to inhabit what are referred to as "ecotone" areas — places along wood lines and fields where one biome transitions into another. One source tells me that skinks actually like areas that have been cleared by burning, so they are animals more than willing to step in and re-start the ecology of scarred environments.

The skink I discovered perusing my files is also called the "blue-tailed" skink when young, and the "red-headed" skink when it reaches maturity. Their colors tend to change or fade as they age, and they become more and more brown as they get older, not unlike an old sun-worshipping beachcomber.

They can reach up to nine inches in length and have been known to live over six years, relatively long in the reptilian world. A bit of red emerges along their heads when they leave their juvenile days behind them, thus their adult names.

I have to admit that I am more than hopeful that this particular skink has no plans to return to his spot under my writing table, and if he does, that he is a he and not a she. Female skinks lay eggs under stones and logs and then nest with them, often turning the eggs to keep them evenly warm and urinating near them to keep the nesting area humid. Determining the gender of skinks is difficult, so let's just hope my skink was just out for a night of gnat-hunting, that I have scared him straight, and there'll be no more forays into the cabin.

As I walked out the door a few early evenings ago, I

saw him again as he was catching what was left of the day's sun. He was splayed out on a piece of sandstone near the purple coneflower that grows on the south side of my cabin, so I grabbed my camera and got one fleeting picture of him before he disappeared into the green of my garden.

I am happy and fortunate that my yard and flower beds and woods are places that skinks and butterflies and birds and snakes find hospitable and safe; I do little to discourage our co-existence. But all invitations to live here stop at my door.

I am cheating a bit with the following story. It comes from the time when I was just beginning to feel my way around as a writer, and as you may know, that was fairly late in life. I have never submitted it for publication or worked it into a column, so for this book it is to serve as my final word.

A Fisher of Men

In the hazy dusk of an early Indiana summer night not long ago, I stared into the glowing embers of a campfire, and looked back into time. I had brought my son to a country pond for an evening of fishing with his cousins, but as I sat amid their laughter and storytelling and watched the sun slip off to bed, I wandered toward the past.

My grandfather and I sat around a similar orange glow and often heard the crackle of burning wood a lifetime ago.

In those days I saw him as a great fisherman, a Hoosier version of Hemingway's old man, Santiago, and I swallowed every fish tale he told, every casting tip he taught. I saw his dented tackle box as a treasure chest, and looked forward to the day when he'd hand his battered, sweat-stained straw hat to me so I could fill its wide blue band with the hooks of my lures.

In his younger days, my grandfather was a bit of a hell raiser, that is until he found my grandmother, gave up on homemade brew, and had the first of his meetings with the Holy Spirit. He once spent a night in jail for punching a man in the nose, but by the time I was old enough to truly know him, he flashed little of the fiery temper he once had, and often sprinkled his lessons with the Biblical passages he labored to commit to memory. He taught much more to me than fishing, and on Wednesday nights when I rode between him and my grandmother down a country road to their small white church in town, I knew that he wanted to teach me how to know a caring God. He prayed with a single tanned arm balanced in the air, and I suspect even now that many of those prayers went up for me.

I know most grandfathers are special men. Mine barely made it through the eighth grade, but was a great teacher, whether it be in his sandy garden plot with an open furrow at our feet or on the banks of some shallow stream, its sunfish still darting through my dreams. He worked hard his whole life, his hands calloused and scarred, and he measured the worth of others, not by what they said or owned, but by what they did for their families and friends.

We'd drive off to fish in the early summer mornings and make a day of it, our lunch a few sandwiches wrapped in waxed paper, a thermos of coffee, and a lukewarm bottle of Pepsi. By the heat of the mid-afternoon, my enthusiasm worn down, I'd begin to ask if we could go home, if we could move to another spot, if we could nap under the shade of a tree. Often, he'd tell me that anything worth having was worth the wait, that if fishing taught a man anything, it was to be at peace with his own thoughts.

He was not necessarily quiet, but he taught me to love solitude. He loved to tell stories and laugh at old jokes, often hummed and whistled hymns that sounded warmly familiar to me. I wanted to gab as we fished in our old johnboat, wanted to skip flat stones in the shallows, wanted to wade in the shin-deep coolness and feel the grey-green mud squeeze between my toes. He'd tell me to be still; that all good fishermen could outlast the murky calm of the fish for which he was casting.

My grandfather wasn't always a patient man, but taught me patience in what I did. As a very young man he once threw away his meager savings for a car just because he liked the look of its dashboard, and in the bleak years of the Great Depression, he often jumped from job to job if he'd felt wronged or the itch for change. By the time he was 24, he had buried a wife and a child, knew what it was to be hungry, and seemed to be searching for something in his life.

His longing and wandering came to an end when his new family settled on a windy Parke County hill, and as the years tumbled past he came to believe that God could work in any man. He proved to me that if we wait long enough in our lives that we'll all feel the gentle tug of the Lord's hand, like the pull of a bobber we can feel, even before we can see it move.

In the years since he died, a number of men who knew him have told me what a good man my Grandpa Roy was, that he was the one soul they saw tending to the churchyard grass on hot Saturday afternoons, or that he was the one most likely to show up at the nursing home to visit old friends. At his worst, they recalled him to be a dangerous driver.

Now, nearly 25 years after his death, all I have of my grandfather besides a heart of memories is his old green fly rod, a few hand tools, and his Bible. Through the latter, I discovered that he couldn't spell very well, that he often underlined favorite passages, and that late in life high blood pressure reduced his handwriting to a scrawl as he scribbled inside its black leather cover the names of the books, chapters, and verses he wanted to remember.

One of those passages is the 16th and 17th verses of the 1st Chapter of the Gospel of Mark: "Now as he walked by the Sea of Galilee, He saw Simon and Andrew his brother casting a net into the sea: for they were fishers. And Jesus said unto them, 'Come ye after me, and I will make you to become fishers of men.'"

As I thumbed through his Bible not so long ago, I found that he still speaks to me. Tucked between two of its onionskin pages was a neatly folded piece of note paper. On it, my grandfather had written: "Just a line from Pa. I did not leave much, so do whatever you want to with it. Anything you want to sell or give away, it is ok. I hope to see you in Heaven with Mother. We will be together again... I will be looking."

When I think of him, I most often see my grandfather in one of two places. He is either standing, rod in hand on the bank of a pond, or he is kneeling at the altar of his church. Samuel Johnson once wrote that a "fishing rod is a stick with a hook at one end and a fool at the other." I disagree; surely Johnson never fished with his grandfather.

Mine was not only a fisherman, but in the footsteps of the carpenter from Galilee, he was a fisher of men. He lived a life of example for me. He proved that a man himself could change and grow, and in the end, gently pull others with him to the shore.

Now it is my son and I who fish together, much in the same way that my grandfather and I did so many years ago. It is so because what I know of fishing came from one man, and I have passed much of that knowledge on to my boy, and to his sister before him. Hopefully, a faith in a God who loves us, will find its way to my grandchildren too.

One could do worse than to be a fisherman, but he can do no better than to be a fisher of men.

Mike Lunsford